This is a photo taken of the "Garlepp Boys" in the 1800's. Unfortunately I don't have the names to go with the faces. But what a find!

I have been researching my family history for over 30 years. I am always finding something new, no matter how finished I think I am. I love the process of researching and putting the puzzles together.

We don't always find rainbows and unicorns in our histories, actually the opposite is more true. Many of our histories are sad and even tragic. But this is what makes us, us.

I have tried to be as accurate as I can be, but if you find a mistake then I whole heartedly apologise for this.

Think about my research being the starting point for your own research. Once you start looking, you'll be surprised just how much you can find about your ancestors.

I acknowledge and thank the following Agencies for their generosity in allowing public access to their records.

PROV (Public Records of Victoria)

Trove (State Library of Victoria)

National Archives of Australia

Ancestry.com

If we know where we came
from, we may better know
where to go. If we know
who we came from,
we may better
understand who we are

Contents

Carl Garlepp was born 15 January 1817 in Prenzlau, Brandenburg, Preußen. Prenzlau is about 116 kilometres from Berlin. His parents were Martin Freidrich Garlepp (1787-1840) and Hanne Caroline Freiderike Christine Garlepp (nee Freiherrn) (1790-1835)

The name Garlepp has been spelt a few different ways. Garliep, Garlieb, etc.

Carl was baptised on 26 January, 1817 in Prenzlau. Below is a copy of the Baptism registration. Yes, it is probably impossible to read, I apologise for that.

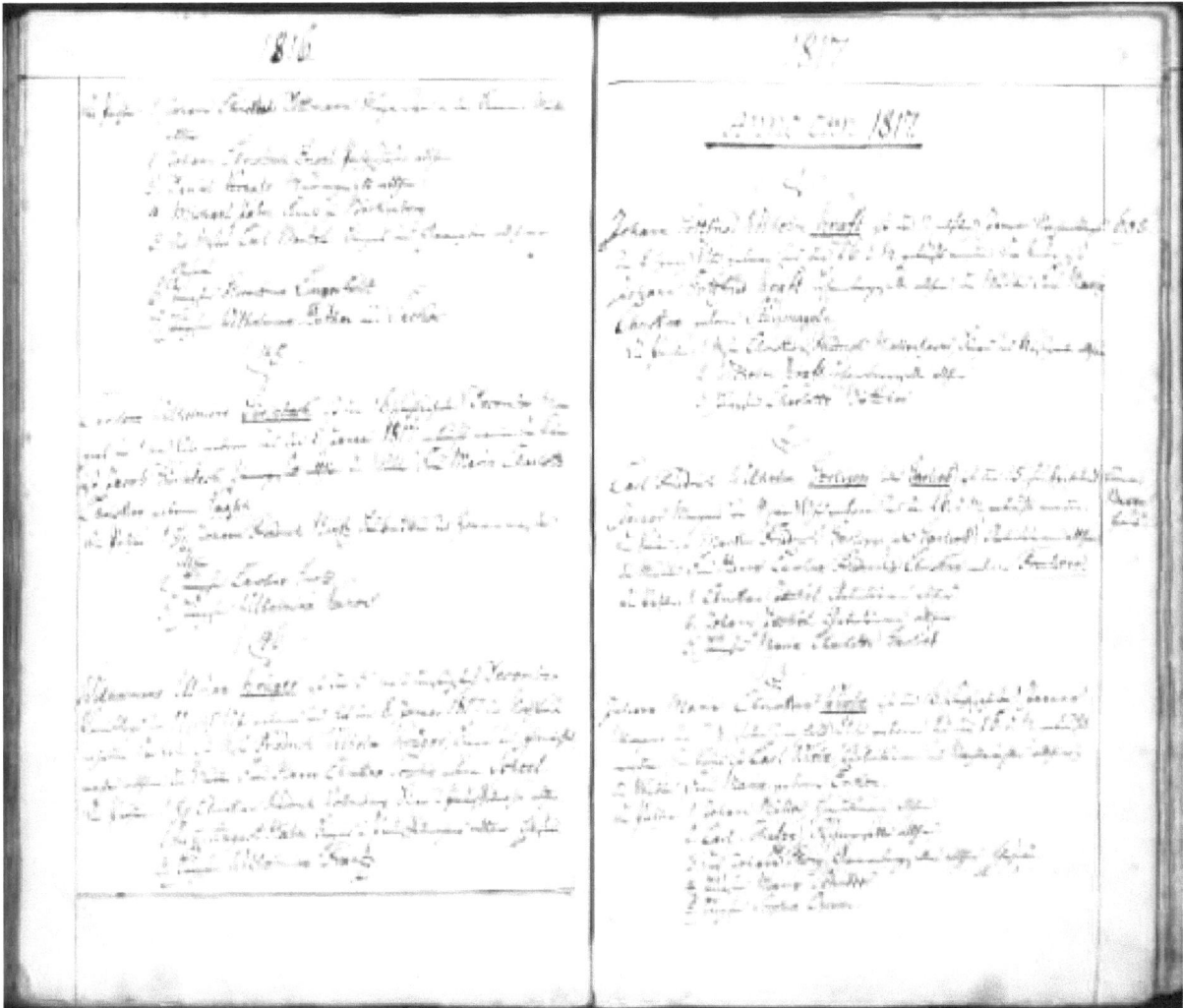

Carl was the second child of the family. His siblings were :

Wilhelmine Marie Charlotte	1812–
August Friedrich	1819–
Henriette Friederike	1822–

On 14 December, 1835, Carl's mother Hanne died and 3 January, 1840 his father Martin died.

Although I can't find the registration, Carl married **Elizabeth Cornelia Brauer** around 1850. He was around 34 at the time and Elizabeth was about 28

Elizabeth Cornelia Brauer was born on 24 May 1821 in Pomorskie, Zachodniopomorskie, Poland, to Maria Brauer and Johann Brauer.

Carl and Elizabeth had five children in Germany. They were:

John Garlepp born before 1851 (died in Prussia)
Fritz Garlepp born before 1851 (died in Prussia)
Carle Erdmann Garlepp born 26 March 1851.
Johann Garlepp born 1853
Wilhelm Garlepp born February 1856.

"ELECTRIC"

On 30 August, 1856, The family set sail aboard The Electric and emigrated to Australia. The journey apparently took a few months but eventually landed in Hobsons Bay, Melbourne on Christmas day 1856. Below is the newspaper notice in The Age on 27 December, 1856. Carl's occupation is listed as a Shepherd.

On 22 January, 1857 the following notice was placed in The Argus.

On 17 February, 1857 the following notice was placed in The Argus.

Apparently around 70,000 people migrated from Germany in the 1800's. The reasons are the same as most mass migration…. Not just Religious and political reasons, but real physical ones such as lack of access to resources.

Carl, or as he had now become known as, Charles and Elizabeth were living in the Somerton / Craigieburn area, after their arrival in Victoria. This is about 20 to 30 kilometres north of Melbourne. There were already a few German immigrants settled around the area, which would have been a comfort to the family.

Charles and Elizabeth had 3 children here:

Hermann Garlepp	(1859–1931)
Henry (Heinrich) Garlepp	(1861–1916)
Ernest Edward Garlepp	(1864–1936)

In January, 1864 Charles bought 55 acres of farm land in the area. Below is the notice in the Leader newspaper dated 30 January 1864, showing that Charles paid 2 pounds 4 shillings for lot 28.

WEDNESDAY'S SALE.
COUNTRY LOTS.

County of Bourke, parish of Yuroke, situated west of the main Sydney roads, at and near the Somerton road, and sixteen miles north of Melbourne. Upset price, £1 per acre for unimproved lots. Lot 23, 25a. 0r. 2p., no offer ; 24, 40a. 3r. 34p., £1 per acre, C. Blakey ; 25, 47a. 3r. 16p., £1 14s do, C. Blakey ; 26, 34a. 0r. 30p., £1 1s do, C. Blakey ; 27, 48a. 3r., 6p., £2 4s do, C. Garlepp ; 28, 55a. 3r. 17p, £2 7s do, C. Blakey ; 29, 54a. 2r. 6p., £1 16s do, C. Blakey ; 30, 42a. 0r. 38p., £2 4s do, C. Blakey ; 31, 39a. 2r. 26p., £5 1s do, John Cameron ; 32, 21a. 3r. 6p., £1 16s do, Samuel Clifford; 33, 26a. 2r. 25p., £2 14s do, Samuel Clifford ; 34, 27a. 2r., £1 17s do, Anthony Harrison ; 35, 27a. 2r., £2 1s do, Anthony Harrison ; 36, 27a. 2r., £1 12s do, J, Kernan ; 37, 28a, 1r. 12p., £1 11s do, J. Dan. Total amount realised, £1307 7s 10s.

According to the 1870 rate book, Charles paid rates on a property in Somerton with a full net annual value of 17 pounds.

According to the 1871 rate book, Charles paid rates on a property with a house in Somerton, with a full net annual value of 17 pounds.

According to the rate book for 1872, Charles paid rates on a 48 acre property in Somerton. The Full Net annual value of the property was 15 pounds.

In 1873 Charles and Elizabeth's son Charles, was married to Christiana Gunther in Benalla. Christiana was also born in Germany, around 1855 to August Philip Gunther (1832-1876) and Eliza Bruhn (1839-1923)

From the records, Charles junior and Christiana were living in Violet Town, where they had the following children:

George Garlepp	1874-1919
Annie Caroline Garlepp	1877-1943
Emma Elizabeth Garlepp	1879-1904

It was somewhere between 1873 and 1875 that Charles and the family had moved to Tamleugh, a small town about 17 kilometres from Violet Town, Victoria.

In 1875 Charles appeared in court, charged by Daniel Sullivan for 31 cattle trespassing on his property. The case was adjourned then dismissed. Here is a newspaper article that talks about it. (Ovens and Murray Advertiser dated 27 February, 1875.)

difficulties, so far completed the edifice as to make it available for public worship.

VIOLET TOWN POLICE COURT.—At this court on Wednesday, before Messrs Gall and Grattan, J.P's., the following business was transacted:—Sullivan v C. Garlepp: Mr McDonald for defendant. The complainant sought to recover £12 8s from defendant for the trespass of 31 head of cattle in his garden. In cross-examination he only knew three head to be defendant's property, and further admitted that the garden was unfenced on one side. The case was dismissed with 31s costs. Playford v A. Wakenshaw; illegally

the same being a direct route of many residents to two of the churches.—Placed on estimates. From Charles Garlepp, stating that when the bridge was constructed across the Honeysuckle Creek he gave a piece of land for approach to it, in consideration that the same quantity in the bend of the creek would be returned, and requesting some information respecting the subject.—Referred to engineer, with a recommendation that if found advisable the Government should grant the piece of land applied for in the bend of the creek in lieu of that given for road purposes.

In the North Eastern Ensign, newspaper on 2 April, 1875, it was reported that Charles was having difficulties with the local Benalla Council. A few weeks later on 9 July, 1875, it was reported in the same newspaper that he was still reminding the Council that they hadn't followed up with their promise. The article is shown below.

Charles advertised some of his sheep for sale according to the notice in the "Leader" on 23 September, 1876. Shown Below.

own lands, next year the council would be in a position to put up one which would be for the public good, and independent of any party. From Charles Garlepp, Violettown, reminding the council that the engineer promised to allow him a piece of land in return for what he gave the council to build a bridge across the Honeysuckle Creek, and saying that the neighbours were disputing his boundary on the creek and he wished it defined.—The PRESIDENT said he was promised a small piece of land adjoining his own in return for what he gave the council, it would be well for the Engineer to see and fix the boundary.—Agreed to.

SATURDAY, 30th SEPTEMBER.
At Twelve o'Clock.
Violet Town.
35 Ewes and Lambs, 60 Dry Ewes, 40 Wethers.
H. LINARD, under instructions received from the owner, Mr. Chas. Garlepp, will sell by auction,
The above really choice lot of sheep, all young, in good wool, and in fair condition.
Farmers desirous of obtaining a few good sheep to start with, will do well to attend, as the auctioneer can with confidence recommend them as being worthy of notice.
Sale at noon, at the auctioneer's Yards, High-street, Violet Town.

Charles was granted a lease on his 320 acres in Tamleugh according to the notice int the "Leader" on 24 March 1877. I assume he didn't own that farm.

LEASES UNDER SECTION 20 GRANTED.
George Donathy, Moyston, 150 acres; John Moore, Wibenduck, 96; Robert Hackney, Kaarimba, 319; George Clyne, Karrabumet, 207; Thomas Treahy, Currawa, 319; Charles Currie, Kaarimba, 319; Joshua Oos, Warrenbayne, 190; Charles O'Brien, Katandra, 150; Thomas Black, Burramine, 201; Charles Garlepp, sen., Tamleugh, 320; Johann C. Meyer, Balmattum, 162; Francis M'Cormack, Bungeet, 79;

10

On 19 January, 1882, the Garlepp boys (Ernest, William and John) were in court. I have transcribed below the details because it's hard to read:

"... *Being refines and vagabonds within the meaning of Part III of the Police Offences Statute 1865? To wit: - That they on the 15th January, 1882 at Tamleugh did wilfully and obscenely in a place of public resort thereat expose their persons.*

The three defendents case dismissed not proved Ernest Garlepp, William Garlepp, and Edward Hayes. John Garlepp struck out, not identified. "

On 2 May, 1884, Charles and Elizabeth's son, Ernest Edward married Ellen French (1866-1931) in the St Joseph's Church in Benalla, Victoria.

In 1885, Wilhelm married Sarah Ann French (1867-1835). Sarah was Ellen's sister.

On 27 May, 1886 Henry married Catherine French (1858-1925) Another French sister.

I find it amazing that 3 brothers married 3 sisters. How often do we find that? Oh wait, it seems the O'Halloran's and the French's liked to marry siblings too.

The French girls were the daughters of John French (1833-1917) and Ellen O'Halloran (1833-1903). John was born in Lancashire, England and emigrated to Australia aboard the Pola in 1853 when he was 20 years old. Ellen (1833-1903) was the daughter of Patrick 1797-1891) and Catherine O'Halloran (nee Canavan 1817-1902). Ellen emigrated to Australia in 1854 aboard the China, along with her sisters Mary and Bridget.

Please read the chapters on the French and O'Halloran family's for more information about them. I have also created chapters for each of the children of Carl and Elizabeth.

In 1883 Charles wanted to sell his farm. I found this article in the North Eastern Ensign newspaper on 6 April 1883.

It's a little hard to read. I have transcribed it….

Tuesday, 24th April. At Eleven o'clock. Tamleugh.
Farm of 317 acres, farming implements, stock etc.
Watts and McBean
Have received instructions from Mr Charles Garlepp to sell at auction on the premises at eleven o'clcock.
Farm of 317 acres.
Which is one of the best in the Parish of Tamleugh.
It is well fenced and subdivided and 80 acres have been cultivated. It has a large frontage to the Stony Creek, and there is also a permanent spring on the property, a dwelling house of six rooms, and an orchard well stocked with a variety of fruit trees in full bearing. It is situated within a few yards of the Tamleugh state school, and about six miles from Violet Town, and is well worthy of inspection by those who are desirous of obtaining a first class farm. Also, 70 head of Mixed Cattle, A team of Eight Bullocks, with gear, 4 Horses, Double and Single furrow Ploughs, Horse Dray, Chaffcutter, with horse-power, 2 Reaping Machines, Blacksmith's Tools, Household Furniture, Poultry, etc. Terms at Sale.

From the article, shown to the right, found in the North Eastern Ensign on 27 April, 1883, Charles was successful in selling the farm.

Charles went on to buy a Hotel in Devenish, called the "Farmers Arms" The notice in the North Eastern Ensign on 17 July, 1883 shows him having the successful transfer of the Licence from Patrick L McCullum. See below.

Messrs Watts & M'Bean report having sold on Tuesday last, on account of Mr C. Garlepp, sen., his farm of 314a 2r 39p, in the parish of Tamleugh, to Messrs. William and John M'Donald at £3 3s. 6d. cash ; also the stock and farming implements, for which there was a large attendance of buyers. The competition was brisk, and all was cleared out at good prices.

(3204) will be open for selection on 27th July.

Transfers registered at the Office of Titles.— Mary Faris, Marraweeney, to Humphrey Grattan, Gowangardie ; Patrick L. M'Callum, Devenish, to Chas. Garlepp, Violettown ; Wm. Langford, Yabba, to Yeamon Gunn.

A few months later, Charles had advertised in The Age on 14 August, 1883 that his horse had been lost and he was offering a reward.

THIRTY Shillings Reward.—Lost, from near the railway station, Devenish, bay draught Horse; white stripe down forehead, lump behind shoulders; and black draught Mare, white stripe down forehead three white feet. C. Garlepp, Devenish.

In May, 1884, Charles was charged with aiding and abetting his son John for cruelty to animals. The article in the North Eastern Ensign dated 6 May 1884 is below.

CRUELTY TO ANIMALS.

Police v John Garlepp: charged with cruelty to a horse. Charles Garlepp was charged with aiding and abetting same. Both cases heard together.

Constable Middleditch stated that the accused, John Garlepp, was driving a mare with a very bad shoulder on the 7th of April. John stated Charles Garlepp was the owner of the horse. The elder defendant stated the horse had been in that state for twelve months and he had never been interfered with.

Louis Charles gave corroborative evidence.

The bench were of opinion that geat cruelty had been practised, and fined both accused in the sum of 20s, with 5s costs, or seven days' imprisonment.

[Dr Nicholson here left the bench.]

NUISANCE.

M. Brown, Devenish. Renewal.—
Granted.

J. Rowan, Devenish. Renewal.—
Granted.

C. Garlepp, Devenish. Renewal.—
Granted.

M. O'Connor. Devenish. New
license. Granted.

According to a notice in the Tungamah and Lake Rowan Express and St James Gazette 3 December, 1885, The Licence for the Farmers Arms at Devenish was renewed.

Just 2 days after the above notice there was an advertisement in the Age newspaper (5 December 1885) for the sale of the Hotel at Devenish.

HOTEL, at Devenish, Rail-street, containing 10 rooms, with four-roomed building, detached, stables and loose box. Apply Garlepp, senior, Devenish.

HOTELS, freeholds and leaseholds, Melbourne, all

On February 19, 1886, Charles was also advertising the sale of 2 brick cottages in Benalla. Within the ad it says that Charles wants to devote his time entirely to farming pursuits. As we will find further in the story, the cottages didn't sell for Charles.

Monday, 1st March; 1886.

Watts and M'Bean

HAVE received instructions from Mr Charles Garlepp, sen., to sell by Auction (through their Auctioneer), at the Benalla Hotel, at o'clock,

TWO BRICK COTTAGES,

He must have been having a major change of heart with his new lifestyle choice of victualler.

Each containing four rooms, on land with a frontage of 79 feet 10 inches to Hanna Street, by a depth of 285 feet enclosed with paling fence. In addition to the water being laid on, there is a large underground tank, 80 feet in circumference by a depth of 18 feet.

And in June, 1886 Charles had sold The Farmers Arms to Helen McGrath.

Below is the notice in The North Eastern Ensign 18 June 1886

The above is for positive sale, as the Proprietor intends to devote his attention entirely to farming pursuits and being immediately opposite the Goods Sheds at the Benalla Railway Station, it affords a good chance for railway employees and others to obtain a convenient residence, and to investors a rare opportunity to secure property of ever increasing value.

Charles Garlepp, Farmers Arms, Devenish, to Helen M'Grath. No police opposition. Granted.

Terms—One-third cash; balance on liberal terms.

In the Tungamah and Lake Rowan Express and St. James Gazette, 18 March 1886, we find that Charles is now selling all his household furniture and effects. Here is a transcription:

"Devenish

Important Clearing Sale of Town Allotments

Household Furniture and Effects

Friday 19th March, 1886.

Green and Crockett (W.G. Crockett, auctioneer) are favored with instructions from Mr C Garlepp, whose hotel we have sold, to sell without reserve on the above date at Devenish:

The whole of his furniture and effects consisting of suite in horsehair, chairs, tables, couches, sofas, bedsteads, and bedding, kitchen utensils etc.

Also a valuable allotment of land comprising one acre in the best part of Devenish.. Sale at 11 o'clock am."

To the right is photo of a building in Devenish that according to a sign at the front of its verandah is the Farmers Arms Hotel. Established 1885.

I'm not convinced this is the same building that Charles owned. I'll explain why further in the story.

According to letters submitted by Herman and Charles junior after their fathers death, Charles lived with Herman for about 4 months 2 years prior, which was probably after the sale of the farm. He then lived at Devenish for about a year. He went back to live with Herman because he was unwell. He was suffering from liver issues caused by heavy drinking.

I notice there is no mention of Elizabeth. I cannot find any records of her death, but according to Charles Last Will and Testament, she was still alive at the time of his death.

Charles died at 8am on 2 August, 1886 at his son Hermans home in Lima. On the following pages I will share their testimonies at the inquest. Plus the results of the inquest.

To date, I have not been able to locate the grave.

The photo of the Farmers Arms is a modern photo taken in the last 10 years or so.

Below is photo of the Farmers Arms in Devenish taken in the very early 1900's. Do they look like the same building to you? I'm not convinced.

On the following page there is a newspaper story about The Farmers Arms written in 1901. It talks about a devastating fire.

Lima 4.8.86

Herman Garlepp being duly sworn on oath saith

My name is Herman Garlepp I am son of the deceased I have lived here about two years My Father came to live with me two years ago & lived with me four months He then went to Keep a Hotel in Devenish & lived there about twelve months when he came back to live with me again about six weeks He was then suffering from Liver complaint caused by heavy drinking while he lived at Devenish He has been laid up for the last three weeks & has eat scarcely anything during the last three weeks he did not eat anything for the last three days & died on Monday morning at 8 oclock.

Herman Garlepp

Sworn before me one of Her Majesty's Justices of the peace for the Northern Bailiwick this fourth day of August 1886

Wm Heaney J.P.

Herman Garlepp's sworn testimony in relation to his fathers death.

Transcription of Herman Garlepp's sworn testimony.

Lima 4.8.86

Herman Garlepp being duly sworn on oath saith

My name is Herman Garlepp I am son of the deceased. I have lived here about two years. My father came to live with me two years ago and lived with me four months. He then went to keep a Hotel in Devenish and lived there about twelve months when he cam back to live with me again about six weeks. He was then suffering from liver complaint caused by heavy drinking while he lived at Devenish. He has been laid up for the las three weeks and has eat scarcely anything during the last three weeks he did not eat anything for the last three days and died on Monday morning at 8 o'clock.

Herman Garlepp

Sworn before me one of Her Majesties Justices of the Peace for the Northern Bailwick. This fourth day of August, 1886.

Signature?

Sima 4.8.86

Charles Garlepp. been duly sworn on oath saith My name is Charles Garlepp I am son of the deceased (Charles Garlepp) I live about one hundred yards from my Fathers house I came to live here about six three months ~~distinct~~ ago my Father was then ill. He had been keeping a hotel at Devonish until about two weeks ago when he came to live at Sima He had been drinking heavily for eleven months, Dr Rhome of Kinginoh visited my father about the latter end of February last & stated that he was suffering from Liver complaint caused by an over dose of strong drink & stated that it would cause his death before long. My Father has not been drinking much since he came to live at Sima He has been laid up for the last three weeks, on Thursday night he seemed to take worse & remained that way until his death which took place on Monday morning at eight oclock.

Charles Garlepp

Sworn before me one of her Majesty's Justices of the peace for the Northern Bailiwick this fourth day of August 1886

Wm Heaney J.P

This is Charles Garlepp junior's testimony. I have transcribed it on the following page.

Transcription of Charles Garlepp Junior sworn testimony.

Lima 4.8.86

Charles Garlepp been duly sworn on oath saith my name is Charles Garlepp.

I am son of the deceased (Charles Garlepp). I live about one hundred yards from my fathers houses. I came to live here about three months ago. My father was then ill. He had been keeping a hotel at Devenish until about six weeks ago when he came to lie at Lima. He had been drinking heavily for eleven months. Dr. ??? of ??? vivsited my father about the latter end of February last and stated that he was suffering from liver complaint caused by an over dose of strong drink and stated that it would cause his death before long. My father has not been drinking much since he came to live at Lima. He has been laid up for the last three weeks, on Thursday night he seemed to take worse and remained that way until his death which took place on Monday morning at eight o'clock.

Charles Garlepp

Sworn before me one of Her Majesties Justices of the Peace for the Northern Bailwick. This fourth day of August, 1886.

Signature?

Colony of Victoria }
Northern Bailiwick } Majesterial Inquiry
To Wit }

A majesterial inquiry on behalf
of our Sovereign Lady. the Quan taken at Lima
in the Northern Bailiwick this fourthday of —
August in the year of our Lord one thousand
eight hundred and eighty six before Wm Heaney
esquire one of her Majesty's Justices of the Peace
in and for the said Bailiwick and Colony, upon view
of the body of Charles Garlepp then and there
lying dead, and having duly inquired on the part of our
Lady the Queen, when where how and by what means the said
Charles Garlepp came by his death. do say that the said
Charles Garlepp died at Lima in the said Bailiwick and
Colony on Monday 2nd From from a general
Break down of the Constitution Caused by
heavy drinking
Witness my hand and Iseal this fourth day of August
1886
Wm Heaney J.P. A Justice of the Race as aforesaid

21

This is a copy of Charles Last Will and Testimony, that he created about a year before his death. It basically says that he was a Licenced Victualler in Devenish, Victoria. He left properties in Benalla and Devenish to his wife Elizabeth. (Notice how shaky his signature is!) On the next page I have written a transcription.

Charles Garlepp Last Will and Testament transcription.

"This is the last Will and Testament of me Charles Garlepp of Devenish.

Licenced Victualler.

After payment of my just debts, funernal and testinenaryy expenses I ???? and bequeath ?? my wife Elizabeth Garlepp all my freehold property consisting of land and houses situated in Benalla and Devenish respectively. Together with all the property of any kind with ? ?? be ?? at the time of my death.

An I hereby appoint ...... of ..... executor of this my will on ?? whereof I have hereunto ?? my house the seventeenth day of December in the year of our Lord Eighteen hundred and eighty four.

Charles Garlepp"

The questions marks above are in place of the words I cannot decipher. I cannot decipher the rest after his signature.

Following are some of the documents used for probate.

In the Supreme Court
OF THE COLONY OF VICTORIA

PROBATE JURISDICTION.

IN THE *estate* of *Charles Garlepp* late
of *Devenish* in the Colony of Victoria *timed retailer*
deceased

Rec'd 2/8/86

STATEMENT OF ASSETS AND LIABILITIES.

ASSETS: Real Estate

One acre of land or thereabouts
situate in Hanna Street Benalla
having a frontage of 79ft 10 in
by a depth of 285 ft on which
are erected two brick cottages
let at 5/- per week each   £250

Personal Estate

One horse   £20
Bill of Exchange due
by Andrew Kennedy on
or about March 1887 being
balance of purchase money
of one acre of land at
Devenish   £100

LIABILITIES

T. S. Moore Benalla amount
due on Bill of exchange   £22
J. W. Cunningham, Grocer Benalla   1

Balance for Duty   353

24 Dec 6/86   £353 —

£376   £376

In the Supreme Court
of the Colony of Victoria } — In its Probate Jurisdiction

In the estate of Charles Garlepp
late of Devenish in the Colony of Victoria
Licensed Victualler deceased.

I Hugh Moodie of Benalla in the Colony of Victoria
Agricultural Implement maker make oath and say. —
1   That I am worth the sum of Two hundred and
seventy pounds in the Colony of Victoria over and above what
will pay all my just debts and liabilities. —
2   That my property in the said Colony to the extent of the
said sum consists of Agricultural implements, Engines, and
machinery, situate upon my freehold property in Carrier Street
Benalla which are of the value of Five hundred pounds and upwards.

Sworn at Benalla in the
Colony of Victoria this Second
day of October in the year
of our Lord One thousand eight
hundred and eighty six. —
Before me

                                    H Moodie

S B Hamrock

a Commissioner of the Supreme Court of the Colony of Victoria for taking affidavits

25

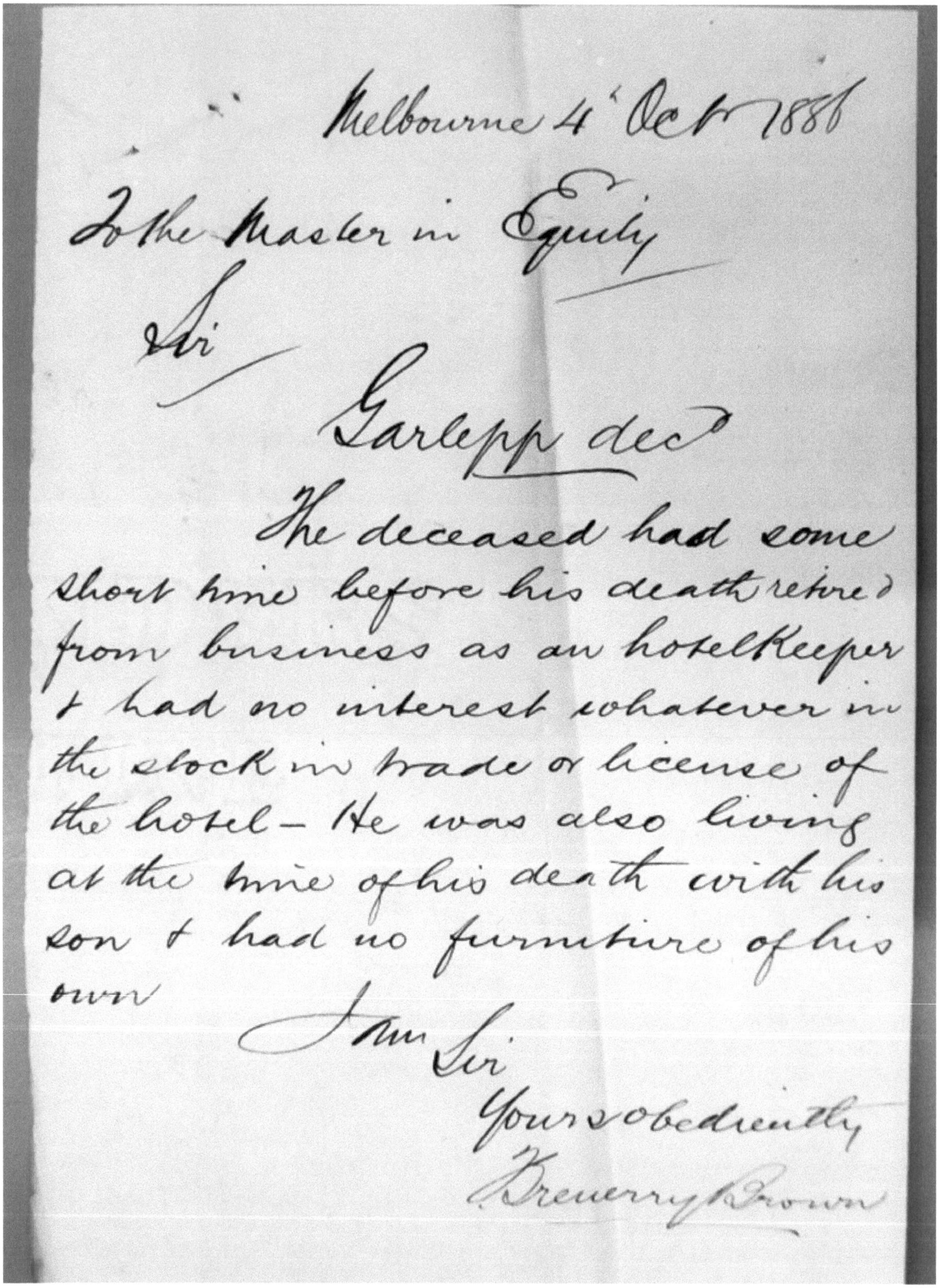

Melbourne 4 Oct 1886

To the Master in Equity

Sir

Garlepp decd

The deceased had some
short time before his death retired
from business as an hotel keeper
& had no interest whatever in
the stock in trade or license of
the hotel — He was also living
at the time of his death with his
son & had no furniture of his
own

I am Sir
Yours obediently
Drewerry Brown

In the Supreme Court
of the Colony of Victoria,

In its Probate Jurisdiction

In the estate of Charles Garlepp
late of Devenish in the Colony of
Victoria Licensed Victualler deceased.

Before The Registrar

The twenty third day of September 1886.

Upon reading the several affidavits of
John Garlepp. Frederick Gregory Brown
and Victor Edward Peter Noriel all sworn
and filed herein Upon reading the will
of the abovenamed deceased I do order
that Letters of Administration, with the
will annexed, be and the same are
hereby granted and committed unto the
said John Garlepp the eldest son of the
said deceased. _____
                    By the Court.

                    [signature]
                    Registrar of Probates

27

In the Supreme Court
OF THE COLONY OF VICTORIA.

IN ITS PROBATE JURISDICTION.

IN THE *estate* of *Charles Garlepp*

late of *Devenish* —————— in the Colony of Victoria

Licensed Victualler deceased.

I *John Garlepp* ——————

of *Lima* —————— in the Colony of Victoria

Farmer —————— make oath and say—

1. That the paper writing hereunto annexed marked "A" contains a true statement of all and singular the real and personal estate of or to which the above named deceased was at the time of h*is* death possessed or entitled and of the values thereof respectively and of the liabilities due thereon and shows a balance of *three hundred and fifty three pounds*

which is the net value of the said real and personal estate.

2. The only person~~s~~ entitled to ~~a distribution of~~ the said estate ~~are~~ *is the widow of the said deceased*

3. That the above named deceased was not possessed of any personal property out of the Colony of Victoria at the time of h*is* decease.

Sworn at *Benalla* in the Colony of Victoria this *twentieth* day of *September* One thousand eight hundred and *eighty six*

John Garlepp

Before me

Guntey Moore

A Commissioner of the Supreme Court of the Colony of Victoria for taking Affidavits.

DESTRUCTIVE FIRE AT DEVENISH.

HOTEL AND TWO BUILDINGS BURNT.

On Friday afternoon shortly before 4 o'clock the Farmers' Arms hotel, Devenish, was discovered by Mr Harry Davis, to be on fire, and in the course of only a few minutes the hotel, a one-roomed building adjoining (used as an office by Mr. Lloyd M'Callum), and Mr. John Willis' saddler's shop next door to it, consisting of a weatherboard building containing the shop, three rooms and the kitchen, were all destroyed. The cause of the fire is a mystery, but it is supposed to have started in the cellar of the hotel. Mr. Davis was preparing to go to Melbourne by the train, and was in his room at the back when he heard a noise like a gun going off. The sound he believed to come from the direction of the cellar. On looking in at the bar he found that it and the bar parlor were all in flames, and he immediately gave the alarm, but owing to the absence of fire-extinguishing appliances the residents were unable to do anything to stay the progress of the flames, and almost as quickly as it takes to say it, the fire had spread to the other buildings named. With difficulty, and more perhaps by good fortune than anything else, the building occupied by Mr Roscoe was saved. The fire was at its height as the train pulled up at the railway station, and provided an imposing spectacle to the passengers. Very little was saved, Mr. Davis having practically nothing, while a small quantity of stock and furniture was taken from Mr Willis' shop, but the hasty manner in which it was removed caused it to be considerably damaged. The hotel building was owned by Mrs Griffiths, and was insured, it is believed, for £280, but that fact has not yet been definitely ascertained. Mr. Davis himself, had his stock and furniture insured in the Lion office for £100, but that will by no means recoup him for his loss, as besides the contents of the hotel he had £57 in gold and notes burnt. This money he intended to take to Melbourne with him, and he left it in some portion of the bar just as he was preparing to get ready. Mr. Jno. Willis had his stock insured in the Colonial Mutual office for £100, and the house was insured in the same office for £200. Mr. Joseph M'Cluskey, a boarder at the hotel, lost a box and a quantity of wearing apparel, which had been left in the room.

Mr. Joseph Hooper, blacksmith, of Devenish, met with a serious accident, which was partly the result of the fire. He was driving from Thoona to Devenish in a gig, and when within a mile of the latter place he noticed the fire, and commenced to hurry up. A stump in the middle of the road was unnoticed by him, and the gig striking it tilted, and he was thrown heavily out on to the road on his head. The vehicle then righted itself, and the horse bolted into Devenish, the gig being a complete wreck at the end of the journey, while the horse was badly crippled. Mr. Hooper had no bones broken, but was much bruised about the head and body. He is now, we are pleased to say, progressing favorably.

This article was in the Benalla Standard on 10 December 1901.

It talks about the devastating fire at the Farmers Arms.

The Next Generations

We have looked at Carl and Elizabeth Garlepp, who were my 3x great grandparents, and how they came to Australia, lived in Victoria, farmed, raised children, ran a pub and eventually died. We've seen that Carl changed his name to be more English sounding, as did his children.

Now I would like to show you what I have found on his children and their descendants. Some of the information can be quite confronting, but we don't all have fairytale families. I like to look at the struggles as well as the celebrations. I am sure there is a lot of information missing, however, I urge you to use my research as a starting point and add to it. Genealogy in my opinion is a journey and there is always more to discover.

I have set the chapters out by each one of Charles and Elizabeth's children and followed their children as far as I can, using publicly known information.

If we know where we came from, we may better know where to go. If we know who we came from, we may better understand who we are

Carle Erdman Garlepp (Charles Junior)

Carle Erdman Garlepp was born on 26 March 1851, in Hohen Mocker, Demmin, Prussia. He was the third child to be born to Carle (Charles) Garlepp and Elizabeth Cornelia Garlepp (nee Braur). His two older siblings were Fritz and Johan both born and died before Carle was born.

In 1856, when Carle was just 5 years old, he emigrated to Australia with his parents and younger brothers Wilhelm and Johan aboard the "Electric".

Here is a picture of the part of the passenger list where their names and ages are registered.

Carle's parents settled in the Somerton, Victoria area. There were a few German settlements spread around the area and I imagine the family would have sought out their company. However, learning the English language would have been necessary. Carle soon became known as Charles Junior and he most probably attended the local school,

The Somerton School opened as a national school in 1850. When it opened it was called Yuroke School. The first schoolhouse was a brick building with shingle roof. There were two rooms for the head teacher to live in.

The picture below (courtesy of the State Library, Victoria) is of an unidentified school of the 1860's. It matches the description above, so may have looked very much like our Somerton School.

In 1873 Charles married Christiana Gunther in Benalla, Victoria.

Christiana, according to her naturalisation information, was born in Demmin, Germany in 14 December, 1853 and arrived aboard the Albatron or Albatros in January 1870. According to her death certificate her father was August Gunther. I think that the informant was wrong, I am pretty sure that August was her brother and that Friedrich Christoph Günther (1807-1870) was her father. Friedrich was married to Johanna Kummerow, Christiana's mother (1805-?) on 29 November, 1832. Christiana had the following siblings:

August Phillip Gunther	1832–1876
Johanna Fredericka Gunther	1836–1897
Maria Sophia or Christine Maria Sophie (Friedericke) Gunther	1836–1897
Friedrich Gunther	1838–1928
Karl Christian Gunther	1841–1919
Friederike Christine Johanne Gunther	1846–1903
Therese Auguste Christiane Günther	1846–1903

Friederich was buried in the Westgarthtown cemetery. There is no further information on Johanna. Westgarthtown is a German settlement that was established in the 1850's.

Around the same time that Charles and Christiana married, Charles parents moved the family to Tamleugh, Victoria.

Charles and Christiana had the following children:

George Garlepp	1874–?	Born in Violet Town
Annie Caroline Garlepp	1877–1943	Violet Town
Emma Elizabeth Garlepp	1879–1904	Tamleugh

On 30 June, 1891, Charles was fined 3 shillings 6 pence, for not sending Annie and Emma to school.

In 1897 Annie Caroline, the second child of Charles and Christiana, married John Driscoll (1867-1934). The 1903 Electoral Roll has Annie and John Driscoll living in Atkinsons Road, Beechworth. John's occupation is listed as Labourer.

Annie and John Driscoll had the following children:

Charles John Driscoll	1897–1983
George Henry Driscoll	1900–1980
Annie Elizabeth Driscoll	1903–1970
Frederick William Gordon Driscoll	1904–1980
Albert James Driscoll	1905–1977
Ethel Maud Driscoll	1907–1981
Irene Myrtle Driscoll	1909–1999

On 24 October, 1902 Emma Elizabeth, Charles and Christiana's youngest child, married William George Dauubenthaler. On 7 July, 1904 they had a son:

William George Daubenthaler   1904-1938

Two days after giving birth, Emma died. Below is a notice placed in the North Eastern Ensign on 29 July 1904.

> whom deceased was greatly beloved.
>   Another death occurred on Tuesday last the victim being Mrs Emma Elizabeth, wife of Mr Wm. J. Daubenthaler, of Swanpool. Death was the outcome of confinement, the deceased having given birth to a child some days previously. The deceased, aged 23½ years, was a native of Tamleugh, in the Euroa district, and was a daughter of Mr Chas. Garlepp, of Swanpool, a well-known and respected resident of that parish. The late Mrs Daubenthaler was a woman of a very kind disposition and was greatly esteemed by those who knew her. Her remains were interred in Benalla cemetery yesterday, the Rev. W. J. Parkes officiating at the grave and Mr Hanlon acting as undertaker
>   The death is also recorded of Mrs Tomkins, a widow, who lived once in Benalla.

William George went on to marry Ellen Timms around 1908 and went on to have a further 3 children:

Henry Edgar Daubenthaler   1909–1967
Charlotte Mary Daubenthaler   1911–1987
Jessie Agnes Daubenthaler   1914–1922

Sometime before 1904, Charles and Christiana had moved to Swanpool, Victoria. In the City Directory he is listed as a grazier.

In September, 1905, George, Charles and Christiana eldest son was trying to obtain 320 acres in the parish of Toorour. The following notices were in the Benalla Standard on 8 September 1905 and 21 September, 1905

> LOCAL LAND BOARD.
>   Schedule of applications to be considered by a Land Board to be held at the Land Office, Benalla, on Tuesday. September 19th, 2 p.m.:—To Show Cause—Parish of Rothesay, Chas. Wicker, 30 acres; parish of Tatong. H. Kennedy, jun., 605 acres, Jas. Kennedy, 675 acres; parish of Taminick S. and W. C. Bain, 457 acres; parish of Lurg, Jas. Kelly, 553 acres; parish of Goomalibee, H. V. Hill, 172 acres; parish of Boweya, C. H. Knight, 49 acres; parish of Myrrhee, 224 acres, E. R. W. Cryer; parish of Toorour, 320 acres, Geo. Garlepp.
>   C. J. TATTAM,
>   Land Officer.
>   Land Office,
>   Benalla, 5th September, 1905.

> E.   R.
> LOCAL LAND BOARD.
>   SUPPLEMENTARY LIST.
>   Schedule of applications to be heard by a Land Board at the Land Office, Benalla, on Tuesday, October 4th, at 2 p.m.
>   TO SHOW CAUSE.
> George Garlepp, 320 acres, Toorour.
>   C. J. TATTAM,
>   Land Officer.
>   Benalla, 21st September, 1904.

36

and Tungamah 46.

GAZETTE NOTICES.—The following notices appeared in last Wednesday's issue of the "Government Gazette":—Application for lease under section 157 of the Land Act 1901 approved: Ernest Dick, Caniambo, 50 acres, Gowangardie; under section 44 of the Land Act 1890, Jas. N. Ford, 109 acres, Moorngag; under section 61 of the Land Act 1898, Wm. G. M'Monigle, 610 acres, Glenrowan. Permit to occupy under section 54 of the Land Act 1901: James Bowler, Tolmie, 322 acres, Dueran. Applications under section 20 of the Land Act 1869 for the issue of Crown grants: A. Sinclair, 320 acres, Ruffy; Jas. H. Boyle, 139 acres, Gowangardie; Edward Moak, 175 acres, Dueran East; Geo. Black, 303 acres, Nillahcootie, do. under section 44 of the Land Act 1890, J. H. Boyle, 50 acres and 61 acres, Gowangardie. Transfer of lease registered at the Office of Titles: Jno. Garlepp to Wm. Geo. Daubenthaler, Benalla, 67 acres, Lima,

In 1905 Charles brother John transferred the lease of 67 acres to William George Daubenthaler, Emma's husband. Here is the notice in the Benalla Standard 8 September, 1905

HEARINGS AGAINST FORFEITURE, &c. JULY.		
		Acres.
26.—Horsham, Edwin Eldridge, Connangorach		136
26.—Horsham, Elizabeth Eldridge, Connangorach and Daahl		996
26.—Horsham, Edwin Eldridge, Connangorach		100
26.—Benalla, George Garlepp, Toorour		320

The Australasian reported on 23 July 1904 that there was a Hearing against Forfeiture on George's 320 acres. (above)

On 1 August, 1906, George was arrested for Insulting Behaviour and remanded to Beechworth.

There was an account in the Benalla Standard on 3 August, 1906. (on the right)

INSULTING BEHAVIOR.—On Wednesday three residents of the Lima district brought into Benalla George Garlepp, aged 28 years. He was strapped down to a board, and, according to their statement, he had been flashing a gun about, and threatened at his house to do injury to various people, and eventually they had to resort to the course stated. Garlepp was brought before Mr. W. Blackburne, J.P., on Wednesday afternoon, and remanded to Beechworth for seven days. In the meantime his mental condition will be taken note of.

/ Weekly Times (Melbourne, Vic. : 1869 - 1954) / Sat 18 Aug 1906

LICENSES AND LEASES RE-VOKED OR DECLARED VOID.

It is notified in the "Government Gazette" of 8th August that the undermentioned licenses and leases have been revoked, forfeited, or declared void :— 1785, Daniel Hehir (permit), Trawalla; 581, William Masterton, Hemboka; 259, John Chandler, Golton Golton; 93, J. Barnacle, Tonimbuk; 873, J. Lowry, Edi; 254, J. Clifford, Tambo State Forest; 293, Robert Halligan, Tallangallook; 1704, Frederick Schulz, Belvoir West; 4402, William H. Hawley, Bullioh; 4451, William H. Gidd, Burrowye; 688, George Garlepp, Too-rour; 705, O. A. Ruck, Laanecoorie; 3832, Walter Smith, Boram Boram; 3262, Walter D. Frith, Boram Boram; 3831, Mary E. Smith, Boram Boram; 1878, Helen Storer, Branxholme; 4359, George Grey, Branxholme; 4361, Henry Grey, Branxholme; 4660, Samuel Grey, Branxholme; 1063, George A. Ball, Branxholme; 4006, Janet Annett, Branxholme; 4883, John Saunders, Branxholme; 3833, Hugh Storer, Branxholme; 3352, Fixby Hinchcliffe, Byaduk; 3444, John

On 18 August, 1906 George's Licence or lease on his land was revoked or declared void, according to an article in The Weekly Times.

In 1911, Charles and Christiana were Naturalised. In that year there were 111 people that took the Oath of Allegiance. I found this article published on 31 December, 1911 in the Sydney Times.

COMMONWEALTH NATURALISATION STATISTICS.

("SUNDAY TIMES" SPECIAL MESSAGE.)
MELBOURNE, Saturday Afternoon.

The number of persons naturalised in the Commonwealth during 111 were:—Men, 1811; women, 266; total, 2077; married 1199, single 878. Among the number were:—Germans 813, Swedes 210, Italians 210, Russians (including 20 Poles and 51 Finns) 159, Danes 156, Norwegians 103, Greeks 87, Austrians 76, French 69, North Americans 61, Swiss 42, Dutch 27, Spaniards 26, also Portuguese, Belgians, Roumanians, Turks, Bulgarians, Brazilians, Chilians, Mexicans, Montenegrins, Syrians, and South Sea Islanders, in various numbers from eight down to single individuals.

The figures for the States are:—New South Wales, 565; Victoria, 491; Queensland, 469; West Australia, 282; South Australia, 248; Tasmania, 22. The total for the year ended December 31, 1910, was 1849, and the total for the year ended December 31, 1911, 2077; increase for 1911 being thus 288.

Obtaining the certificate took quite a bit of paperwork. It seems that both Charles and Christiana had their paperwork witnessed by the wrong type of authority and therefore had re apply.

Bureaucracy processes have always been difficult processes to negotiate.

It seems they achieved their positive end result. Over the next few pages I will share copies of all their paperwork so that you can see all the information that was shared.

It makes for interesting reading.

FORM D.

COMMONWEALTH OF AUSTRALIA.

NATURALIZATION ACT 1903.

OATH OF ALLEGIANCE.

1. Name in full. I,¹ *Charles Edmond Garlepp* do swear

that I will be faithful and bear true allegiance to His Majesty King George V.

His heirs and successors according to law. So HELP ME GOD!

Signature *Charles E Garlepp*

CERTIFICATE.

1. Name in full. I, *James William Waight Beaven*

2. Justice of High Court, Judge of Court of State, Police, Stipendiary, or Special Magistrate. a² *Police Magistrate*

do hereby certify that on the *20th* day of *July* 19 *11*

3. Name of applicant. *Charles Edmond Garlepp*

4. Address of applicant. of⁴ *Ferns East* in the State of⁵ *Victoria*

5. Name of State and occupation of applicant. *Laborer* an applicant for a

Certificate of Naturalization appeared before me and took the Oath of Allegiance in

the above form.

Signature *J.W.W. Beaven*

39

COMMONWEALTH of AUSTRALIA.

DEPARTMENT OF EXTERNAL AFFAIRS.

Melbourne, 23rd June, 1911.

IN REPLY
PLEASE QUOTE
No. 11/10500.

Sir,

Referring to your application for
naturalization, I observe that the certificate
attached to the Oath of Allegiance (Form D) has
been signed by a Justice of the Peace, whereas
the Act prescribes that such Oath may only be
taken before a Justice of the High Court, Judge
of Court of any State, Police Stipendiary, or
Special Magistrate. ("Special Magistrate" applies
to the State of South Australia only.)

2.   It will be necessary for you to
take a fresh Oath before one of the Officers
named, and I enclose a form for that purpose.

I have the honour to be,

Sir,

Your obedient Servant,

Acting-Secretary.

Mr C.E.Garlepp,
     Lima East,
          Victoria.

EXTERNAL AFFAIRS.

Melbourne, 23rd June, 1911.

11/10500.

Sir,

Referring to your application for
naturalisation, I observe that the certificate
attached to the Oath of Allegiance (Form D) has
been signed by a Justice of the Peace, whereas
the Act prescribes that such Oath may only be
taken before a Justice of the High Court, Judge
of Court of any State, Police Stipendiary, or
Special Magistrate. ("Special Magistrate" applies
to the State of South Australia only.)

2.   It will be necessary for you to
take a fresh Oath before one of the Officers
named, and I enclose a form for that purpose.

I have the honour to be,

Sir,

Your obedient Servant,

Acting-Secretary.

Mr C.E.Garlepp,
     Lima East,
          Victoria.

"SPRENT VILLA,"
HANNA STREET.

Benalla _19/ 6/ 1911

Secty
Department External Affairs

Sir

Enclosed please find
papers from Charles E Garlepp
and Christiana Garlepp in
reference to application for
certificate of Naturalization
also Oath of Allegiance.
As the latter has to be
signed before a Police
Magistrate instead of a Justice
of Peace, please forward 2
more papers direct to the applicant
(Lima E) to enable
them to attend at the local
Court on the Pm day
Yours Resp.
_____ JP

EA
1/10501

Form A.

COMMONWEALTH OF AUSTRALIA.

Naturalization Act 1903.

No. of Certf. 9328
When Posted 20/9/11

APPLICATION FOR CERTIFICATE OF NATURALIZATION.

TO HIS EXCELLENCY THE GOVERNOR-GENERAL.

1. Name in full. I, Charles Eramar Garlepp

2. Address and occupation. of Lima East, Victoria
hereby apply for a Certificate of Naturalization under the *Naturalization Act* 1903.

2. I am by birth a German

3. Country or "French citizen," &c., as case requires. I arrived in Australia from Germany on the _____ day of _____ in the year 1857 (does not remember only age of age)

4. Country of previous residence.

5. Name of ship. per the _____ and disembarked at the port of Melbourne Victoria

6. State places, and periods in each. Since my arrival in Australia I have resided at Epping Violet Town and Benalla districts

5. I have resided in Australia continuously for a period of two years immediately preceding the date of this Application. Yes

6. I forward herewith a Statutory Declaration setting forth the particulars required by section 6, sub-section 1, paragraph (a) of the said Act. (Wife

7. State whether married or unmarried, and residence of wife. I am married man residing with

8. State number. I have 3 children 2 female 1 male

9. State number of each sex, and where resident.

9. I am not a naturalized subject or citizen of any other country.
Note.—If the Applicant has taken out Naturalization Papers in any other country this statement should be amended accordingly.

10. State the name of the person, and whether he is a Justice of the Peace, Postmaster, Teacher of State School, or Officer of Police. I forward also a certificate signed by _____ Walker JP
of Benalla to the effect that I am known to him, and am a person of good repute.

11. Signature of applicant. Charles Garlepp

Dated at _____ the _____ 190_

PAPERS IN ORDER
PREPARE EXEC. CO. MINUTE

CERTIFICATE
Referred to in paragraph 10 of annexed Application.

1. Full name. I, George James Walker
2. State whether a Justice of the Peace, Postmaster, Teacher of State School, or Officer of Police. Justice of Peace residing at Benalla in the State of Victoria in the Commonwealth of Australia, do certify that
3. Name of Applicant. Charles Eramar Garlepp
an applicant for a Certificate of Naturalization under the *Naturalization Act* 1903, is known to me, and is a person of good repute.

4. Signature. _____ JP

41

VICTORIA.

STATUTORY DECLARATION.

Referred to in Paragraph 6 of annexed application.

I, *Charles Erdman Garleff*

do solemnly and sincerely declare that—

1. My name is *Charles Erdma Garleff*

2. My age is *60* years, and I was born on the *26th* day of *March 1851* in the year *1851* at *Hohenmoeker* in the *Pommern* in the Country of *Prussia*

3. My occupation is that of *Laborer*

4. My place of residence is *Lima East* in the State of *Victoria* in the Commonwealth of Australia.

5. I have been resident in Australia for *54* years.

6. I intend to settle in the Commonwealth.

I make this solemn declaration conscientiously believing the same to be true, and by virtue of the provisions of an Act of the Parliament of Victoria rendering persons making false declarations punishable for wilful and corrupt perjury.

Made and declared before me at *Benalla* this *13* day of *June* 190*7*

C. Charles Garleff

Walker J.P.

It is particularly requested that the writing, especially of the names of persons and places, be plain and legible.

Form D.

COMMONWEALTH OF AUSTRALIA.

NATURALIZATION ACT 1903.

OATH OF ALLEGIANCE.

I, *Charles E Garleff* do swear that I will be faithful and bear true allegiance to His Majesty King ~~Edward VII~~ *George V* His heirs and successors according to law. So help me God!

Signature *C Charles Garleff*

CERTIFICATE.

I, *George James Walker J.P.* of *Lima East & Benalla* do hereby certify that on the *15th* day of *June* 1911 *Charles Erdman Garleff* of *Lima E* in the State of *Victoria* occupation *Laborer* an applicant for a Certificate of Naturalization appeared before me and took the Oath of Allegiance in the above form.

Signature *Walker J.P.*

42

LM D.

COMMONWEALTH OF AUSTRALIA.

NATURALIZATION ACT 1903.

OATH OF ALLEGIANCE.

1. Name in full.   I, *Christiana Garlepp* do swear

that I will be faithful and bear true allegiance to His Majesty King George V.

His heirs and successors according to law. So HELP ME GOD!

Signature   *Christiana Garlepp*

CERTIFICATE.

1. Name in full.   I, *James William Waight Beavers*

2. Justice of High Court, Judge of Court of State, Police, Stipendiary, or Special Magistrate.   a *Police Magistrate*

do hereby certify that on the *20th* day of *July* 19*11*

3. Name of applicant.   *Christiana Garlepp.*

4. Address of applicant.   of *Alma East* in the State of *Victoria*

5. Name of State and occupation of applicant.   *Married Woman* an applicant for a

Certificate of Naturalization appeared before me and took the Oath of Allegiance in

the above form.

Signature   *J W Beavers*

Received from the Secretary to the Department of External Affairs

Certificate of Naturalization No. _12222_

Signature _Christiana Garlopp_

Date _10 of October 1911._

C.4216

EXTERNAL AFFAIRS.

11/10501

Melbourne, 23rd June, 1911.

Sir,

Referring to your application for naturalization, I observe that the certificate attached to the Oath of Allegiance (Form D) has been signed by a Justice of the Peace, whereas the Act prescribes that such Oath may only be taken before a Justice of the High Court, Judge of Court of any State, Police Stipendiary, or Special Magistrate. ("Special Magistrate" applies to the State of South Australia only.)

2.   It will be necessary for you to take a fresh Oath before one of the Officers named, and I enclose a form for that purpose.

I have the honour to be,

Sir,

Your obedient Servant,

Acting-Secretary.

epp,

a.

FORM A.

EXTERNAL AFFAIRS 10501 1911

COMMONWEALTH OF AUSTRALIA.

Naturalization Act 1903.

No. of Certif _12225_

When Passed _20.9.11_

APPLICATION FOR CERTIFICATE OF NATURALIZATION.

TO HIS EXCELLENCY THE GOVERNOR-GENERAL.

1. Name in full.   1. I, _Christiana Garlepp_
2. Address and occupation.   of _Lima East_

hereby apply for a Certificate of Naturalization under the *Naturalization Act 1903.*

3. State "German subject" or "French citizen," &c., as case requires.   2. I am by birth a _German_
4. Country of previous residence.   3. I arrived in Australia from _Germany_ on the _____ day of _January_ in the year _1870_
5. Name of ship.   per the _Collation_ and disembarked at the port of _Melbourne_

6. State places, and periods in each.   4. Since my arrival in Australia I have resided at _Violet Town Epping and Benalla District_

5. I have resided in Australia continuously for a period of two years immediately preceding the date of this Application. — _Yes_

6. I forward herewith a Statutory Declaration setting forth the particulars required by section 6, sub-section 1, paragraph (a) of the said Act.

7. State whether married and unmarried, and residence of wife.   7. I am _married woman_
8. State number of each sex, and where resident.   8. I have _3_ children _2 Female 1 Male_

9. I am not a naturalized subject or citizen of any other country.

NOTE.—If the Applicant has taken out Naturalization Papers in any other country this statement should be amended accordingly.

10. State the name of the person, and whether he is a Justice of the Peace, Postmaster, Teacher of State School, or Officer of Police.   10. I forward also a certificate signed by _J Walker of Benalla_ to the effect that I am known to him, and am a person of good repute.

11. Signature of applicant.   11. _Christiana Garlepp_

Dated at _15_ day the _June_ 190_1_

C.6307.

PAPERS IN OFFER 17/6/11

PREPARE EXEC. MINUTE

CERTIFICATE

Referred to in paragraph 10 of annexed Application.

1 Full name. I, *George James Walker*

2 State whether a Justice of the Peace, Postmaster, Teacher of State School, or Officer of Police. a *Justice of Peace* residing at *Benalla* in the

State of *Victoria* in the Commonwealth

of Australia, do certify that 3 Name of Applicant. *Christian Garleff*

an applicant for a Certificate of Naturalization under the *Naturalization Act* 1903, is known to me, and is a person of good repute.

4 Signature. *G H Walker J.P.*

FORM D.

COMMONWEALTH OF AUSTRALIA.

NATURALIZATION ACT 1903.

OATH OF ALLEGIANCE.

1 Name in full. I, *Christiana Garleff* do swear

that I will be faithful and bear true allegiance to His Majesty King ~~Edward VII~~ *George V*

His heirs and successors according to law. So HELP ME GOD!

Signature *Christiana Garleff*

CERTIFICATE.

1 Name in full. I, *George James Walker J.P.*

2 Justice of High Court, Judge of Court of State, Police, Stipendiary, or Special Magistrate. a *Justice of Peace*, do hereby certify that on the *15th* day of *June* *1911*

3 Name of applicant.

4 Address of applicant. of *Swanpool* in the State of *Victoria*

5 Name of State and occupation of applicant. *Married Woman* an applicant for a

Certificate of Naturalization appeared before me and took the Oath of Allegiance in

the above form.

Signature *G H Walker J.P.*

VICTORIA.

STATUTORY DECLARATION.

Referred to in Paragraph 6 of annexed application.

1 Name in full. I, *Christiana Garleff*

do solemnly and sincerely declare that—

1. My name is *Christiana Garleff J.P.*

2. My age is *57* years, and I was born on the *1st*
day of *December* in the year *1853*

2 Name of city, town, or locality. at *Demmin* in the

3 County, state, department, province, or as the case may be. in the

in the Country of *Germany*

3. My occupation is that of *Residing with Husband*

4 Full address. 4. My place of residence is *Swanpool* in the State of
Victoria in the Commonwealth of Australia.

5. I have been resident in Australia for *over 40* years.

6. I intend to settle in the Commonwealth. —

I make this solemn declaration conscientiously believing the same to be true,
and by virtue of the provisions of an Act of the Parliament of Victoria rendering
persons making false declarations punishable for wilful and corrupt perjury.

Made and declared before me at
Benalla
this *15th* day of
June *1911*

Christiana Garleff

G H Walker J.P.

It is particularly requested that the writing, especially of the names of persons and places,
be plain and legible.

In the 1912 City Directory Charles is living in Swanpool and in the 1914 City Directory is says he was living in Lima South as a farmer.

Also in 1912, Charles' brother, John died.

According to the Electoral records, Charles and Christiana were still living in Swanpool in 1913 and his occupation is labourer.

In 1916, Charles brother, Henry died .

In the Electoral records of 1919, we find that Charles and Christiana are now living in Wedge Street, Benalla and he is working as a labourer. He is

It seems that Charles' son, George remained in the area, working as a farmer and never married. His death wasn't registered, but I've heard that he died in 1919. This needs further investigation.

Charles and Christiana stayed in Wedge Street, until Charles death 2 December, 1925. Charles was 74 when he died. He was buried in the Benalla Cemetery.   His obituary is below and I have transcribed it for easier reading.

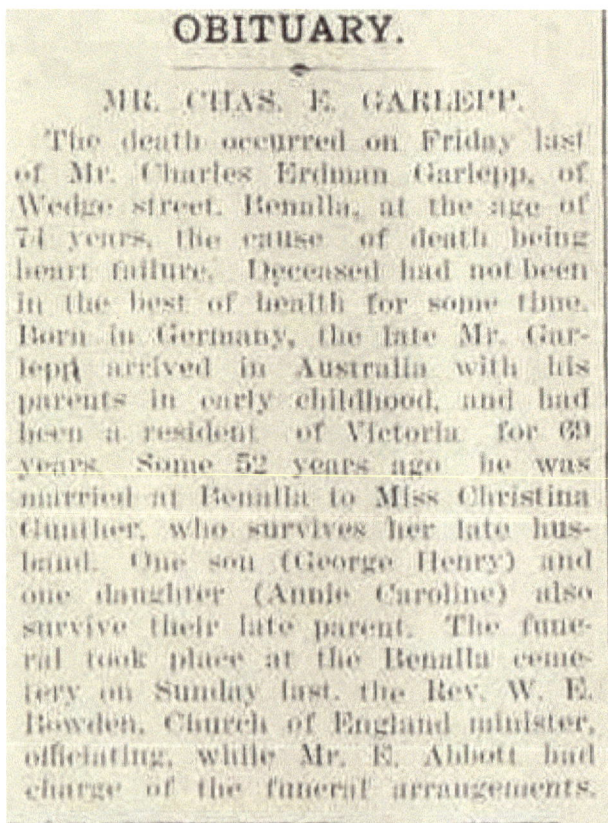

OBITUARY.

MR. CHAS. E. GARLEPP.

The death occurred on Friday last of Mr. Charles Erdman Garlepp, of Wedge street, Benalla, at the age of 74 years, the cause of death being heart failure. Deceased had not been in the best of health for some time. Born in Germany, the late Mr. Garlepp arrived in Australia with his parents in early childhood, and had been a resident of Victoria for 69 years. Some 52 years ago he was married at Benalla to Miss Christina Gunther, who survives her late husband. One son (George Henry) and one daughter (Annie Caroline) also survive their late parent. The funeral took place at the Benalla cemetery on Sunday last, the Rev. W. E. Bowden, Church of England minister, officiating, while Mr. E. Abbott had charge of the funeral arrangements.

Transcription of Obituary

"OBITUARY

Mr Chas E. Garlepp

The death occurred on Friday last of Mr Charles Erdman Garlepp, of Wedge Street, Benalla, at the age of 74 years, the cause of death being heart failure. Deceased had not been in the best of health for some time. Born in Germany, the late Mr Garlepp arrived in Australia with his parents in early child-hood, and had been a resident of Victoria for 69 years. Some 52 years ago he was married at Benalla to Miss Christina Gunther, who survives her late husband. One son (George Henry) and one daughter (Annie Caroline) also survive their late parent. The funeral took place at the Benalla cemetery on Sunday last. The Rev. W. E. Bowden, Church of England minister officiating, while Mr E Abbott had charge of the funeral arrangements."

Christiana moved into an Aged Care facility called Millers Homes in Benalla. She died at the age of 87.

OBITUARY

MRS CHRISTINA GARLEPP.

The death took place at the Miller Homes on Friday last, of Mrs Christina Garlepp, an old resident of the town, at the age of 87 years. The late Mrs Garlepp, who is a daughter of the late Augustus and Fredrica Gunther, was born at Dottengem, Germany, and came to Victoria when 14 years of age. She was married at Benalla 48 years ago, to Mr Charles Erdmann Garlepp, who pre-deceased her 16 years ago. She reared a family of three, George (deceased), Annie Caroline (Mrs Driscoll, Beechworth), and Emma Elizabeth (deceased). Following a short service at Holy Trinity Church on Sunday last, the cortege left for the Benalla cemetery, where interment took place. Rev. C. M. Kennedy officiated at the church and the graveside. The coffin was carried by Messrs G. Driscoll, H. Clarke, A. Ward, W. Daubenthaler, J. Driscoll and W. Horsburgh. The pall was supported by Messrs J. Nelson, W. Clarke, R. J. Hadden, G. Jensen, G. Lucas and A. Jensen. The funeral arrangements were in the hands of Mr H. A. Abbott.

Below is a picture of their grave at Benalla Cemetery.

DEATHS in the District of Benalla in Victoria, Registered by M. G. O'Shea

1	474
Description—	
2 (1) When and where Died ...	15th November 1941. No 9 Miller's Homes, Benalla. Shire of Benalla. County of Delatite.
(2) Usual Place of Residence ...	As above
3 Name and Surname	Christiana Garlepp.
Occupation	Home Duties.
4 Sex and Age	Female. 87 years
5 (1) Cause of Death	(a) Heart failure (b) Asthenic (b) Carcinoma (Intestinal)
(2) Duration of last Illness ...	(c) 6 months
(3) Legally qualified medical practitioner by whom certified ... and	Dr. A. L. McCardel.
(4) When he last saw Deceased ...	15th November 1941.
6 Name and surname of Father and Mother (maiden name, if known), with Occupation	Augustus Gunther Storeman Ferdrica Gunther. M.N. Not known.
7 Signature, Description, and Residence of Informant	*[signature] E A Abbott Authorised Agent Benalla.*
8 (1) Signature of Registrar ... (2) Date ... ... and (3) Where Registered	*[signature] M G O'Shea* 17th November 1941. Benalla.
If burial registered—	
9 When and where Buried ...	16th November 1941. Benalla cemetery
Undertaker by whom certified ...	E. A. Abbott.
10 Name and Religion of Minister, or names of Witnesses of burial ...	Rev. U. M. Kennedy. Church of England clergyman
11 Where born, and how long in the Australian States, stating which	Dottengem. Germany. 73 years Victoria
If deceased was married—	
12 (1) Where ... ... and (2) At what Age ... ... and (3) To Whom... ... ... (4) Conjugal Condition at Date of Death	Benalla. 19 years Charles Erdman Garlepp. Widow.
13 Issue in order of Birth, the Names and Ages	George Henry (Deceased). Annie Caroline 65 years Emma Elizabeth (Deceased).

In early 1921, Annie Caroline's husband, John Driscoll was in a workplace accident. His leg was amputated as a result, which meant he couldn't work from then on. He was 54 at the time.

Here is an article about the discussion in the Beechworth United Shire Council meeting in regards to compensation. This was printed in the Ovens and Murray Advertiser on 2 April 1921.

I have transcribed the relevant section.

try and get the Monday night train. He moved that the Traders' Association be asked to attend.

The engineer said the suggestion to cut out the Thursday morning train was made subsequent to the motion being carried. It was not in the motion.

Cr Phillips said it had been afterwards agreed not to make this suggestion to the Commissioners.

Cr J. Ferguson said there was nothing in the motion in the report about the Thursday morning train.

The President said he would ask the Traders' Association aal Yackandandah people to support the Monday night train without touching on the Thursday morning train at all. This was agreed to.

ENGINEER'S REPORT.

The report was adopted.

INSPECTOR'S REPORT.

The report was adopted.

QUESTION OF WORKMAN'S COMPENSATION.

Cr Warner asked under what condition they stood in relation to a workman named John Driscoll whose leg was crushed in an accident while he was employed by the Council. He understood half the wages the man got were to be paid. A certain party said the State Insurance Company tried to give this woman (Mrs Driscoll) 10s. If so they had no right to be in the State Company. (Quite right.) He had been spoken to by this woman, and he wanted to know the conditions under which they insured their men. A casual man was only entitled to 10s a week. In other insurance companies it was not so. If the engineer would explain the conditions they would understand it.

Cr Phillips said the ratepayers had a perfect right to know what was being done and he hoped the reporter for the "Ovens and Murray Advertiser" would print every word in big type. He must have got 10s a day and only worked one day when the accident happened and should get 30s a week, for Driscoll was working in Kibell's place and whilst there was relieving Kibell. In the meantime Kibell was not insured. It went on to Driscoll because if Kibell got injured whilst on holidays the State in-

jured whilst on holidays the State insurance Company was not responsible so they saw that Driscoll took Kibell's place and was standing in Kibell's shoes. When this man got hurt an inspector practically tried to get his wife to accept 10s a week and he (Cr Phillips) believed she said she would. This man had the cheek to ask this woman how much her husband gave her a week. Mrs Driscoll was one of the best women in Victoria and had had a rotten hard pull and it was a rotten thing for any man to ask her whether her husband supported her or not. She supported her children and brought them up well. Her husband met with a dreadful accident His leg was crushed and had to be taken off. This inspector from Melbourne actually tried to get her to take 10s a week. The Council should withdraw out of this Company as soon as their premium became due.

The President explained that the reason members of the committee desired this matter kept out of the Press was that they expected a reply from the State Insurance Company before the meeting and in the event of a favourable reply being received all would have been well. As no reply had come forward he favoured every were Cr Phillips said going into the Press.

Cr Vandenberg said this woman had had one of the hardest trials and now if the State Insurance Company would not pay her compensation the Council would have to. They would have to do all they possibly could to get all they could out of the insurance company. They should do all they possibly could to see the woman properly compensated. He would help in every way in and out of the Council.

Cr Warner said there was no use talking, he wanted to know what the agreement was.

Cr O'Neill said it seemed to him they were afraid the Council would have to pay if the insurance company would not. What was the use of insuring at all if there was a doubt about it?

The President said the Council would compel the State Insurance Company to pay what it was liable to pay.

Cr Polmear said Driscoll was employed by the Council to work in Kibell's place and the State Insur-

INSPECTOR'S REPORT.
The report was adopted.
QUESTION OF WORKMAN'S COMPENSATION.

Cr Warner asked under what condition they stood in relation to a workman named John Driscoll whose leg was crushed in an accident while he was employed by the Council. He understood half the wages the man got were to be paid. A certain party said the State Insurance Company tried to give this woman (Mrs Driscoll) 10s. If so they had no right to be in the State Company. (Quite right). He had been spoken to by this woman, and he wanted to know the condition under which they insured their men. A casual man was only entitled to 10s a week. In other insurance companies it was not so. If the engineer would explain the conditions they would understand it.

Cr Phillips said the ratepayers had a perfect right to know what was being done and he hoped the reporter for the Ovens and Murray Advertiser would print every word in bold type. He must have got 10s a day and only worked one day when the accident happened and should get 30s a week, for Driscoll was working in Kibell's place and whilst there was relieving Kibell. In the meantime Kibell was not insured. It went on to Driscoll because if Kibell got Injured whilst on holidays the State insurance Company was not responsible so they saw that Driscoll took Kibell's place and was standing in Kibell's shoes. When this man got hurt an inspector practically tried to get his wife to accept 10s a week and he (Cr Phillips) believed she said she would. This man had the cheek to a ask this woman how much her husband gave her a week. Mrs Driscoll was one of the best women in Victoria and had had a rotten hard pull and it was a rot thing for any man to ask her whether her husband supported her or not. She supported her children and brought them up well. Her hus band met with a dreadful accident. His leg was crushed and had to be taken off. This inspector from Melbourne actually tried to get her to take 10s a week. The council should withdraw out of this company as soon as their premium became due.

The President explained that the reason members of the committee de sired this matter kept out of the press was that they expected a reply from the State Insurance Company be fore the meeting and in the event of a favourable reply being received all would have been well. As no reply had come forward he fa-voured every word Cr Phillips said going into the Press.

Cr Vandenberg said this woman had had one of the hardest trials and now if the State Insurance Company would not pay her compensation the Council would have to. They would have to do all they possibly could to get all they could out of the insurance company. They should doll they possibly could to see the woman properly compensated. He would help in every way in and out of the Council.

Cr Warner said there was no use talking, he wanted to know what the agreement was.

Cr O'Neill said it seemed to him they were afraid the Council would have to pay if the insurance company would not. What was the use of insuring at all if there was a doubt about it?

The President said the Council would compel the State Insurance Company to pay what it was liable to pay.

Cr Polmear said Driscoll was employed by the Council to work in Kibell's place and the State Insurance Company was responsible and would not go to court over it. They did not put any man's name down in their policy. They only paid on a certain amount of wages paid each year.

Annie Caroline died 20 May, 1943. There was a lovely obituary in the Ovens and Murray Advertiser on 2 June 1843.

I have transcribed it below.

Obituary

Mrs Annie C Driscoll

A much respected resident of Beechworth. Mrs. Annie Caroline Driscoll, passed away at the Ovens District Hospital on Saturday last 29th May. Mrs Driscoll, who had been ailing for the past 10 months was a daughter of the late Mr and Mrs C. Garlepp of Benalla and was born at Swanpool 67 years ago. In 1896 she married Mr John Driscoll of Beechworth who died in May 1914. She is survived by the following children: Jack (Orange NSW), George (Beechworth), Annie (Mrs I. Hall Melbourne), Jim (Beechworth) Ethel (Mrs S Plunkett, Fallon) and Irene (Mrs A Ward Beechworth). She also leaves 14 grand children. Much sympathy is expressed for her family at the loss of a loving and devoted mother, who owing to her husband being Incapacitated from work after a serious accident in 1921, brought them up and maintained them for many years. The funeral cortege moved from Christ Church on Monday afternoon last to the Beechworth cemetery.   The Rev A. B. Brown officiating at the graveside. Mr W. Guthrie had charge of the mortuary arrangements.

OBITUARY

MRS. ANNIE C. DRISCOLL.

A much respected resident of Beechworth. Mrs. Annie Caroline Driscoll, passed away at the Ovens District Hospital on Saturday last, 29th May. Mrs. Driscoll, who had been ailing for the past 10 months, was a daughter of the late Mr. and Mrs. C. Garlepp, of Benalla, and was born at Swanpool 67 years ago. In 1896 she married Mr. John Driscoll, of Beechworth, who died in May, 1914. She is survived by the following children: Jack (Orange, N.S.W.), George (Beechworth), Annie (Mrs. L. Hall, Melbourne), Jim (Beechworth), Ethel (Mrs. S. Plunkett, Fallon), and Irene (Mrs. A. Ward, Beechworth). She also leaves 14 grand children. Much sympathy is expressed for her family at the loss of a loving and devoted mother, who, owing to her husband being incapacitated from work after a serious accident in 1921, brought them up and maintained them for many years. The funeral cortege moved from Christ Church on Monday afternoon last to the Beechworth cemetery, the Rev. A. B. Brown officiating at the graveside. Mr. W. Guthrie had charge of the mortuary arrangements.

Charles and Christiana's descendants were:

George Henry Garlepp	1874-1919
Annie Caroline Garlepp	1877-1943
Married	1897
John Driscoll	1867-1934
children	
George Henry Driscoll	1900–1980
married	around 1835
Olive Jane Butters	1906-1970
Charles John Driscoll	1897–?
Annie Elizabeth Driscoll	1903–1970
married	
Leslie Norman Hall	1906-1987
children	
Norman Leslie Hall	-1943
Frederick William Gordon Driscoll	1902-1902
Albert James Driscoll	1905–1977
Ethel Maud Driscoll	1907–1981
married	1935
William Sydney Plunkett	1902-1971
children	
Patricia Plunkett	1936–1994
Sydney Albert Plunkett	1937–2022
John Plunkett	1941–2005
William Plunkett	1945–2005
Irene Myrtle Driscoll	1909–1999
married	1929
Alfred James Ward	1906-1996
children	
Isabel Joan Ward	1929–2020
Margaret Caroline Ward	1941–1999
Lorraine Ward	1943–2010
Freda Ward	
David Ward	
Phyllis Ward	
Ken Ward	
Emma Elizabeth Garlepp	1879-1904
married	1902
William George Daubenthaler	1872–1938
children	
William George Daubenthaler	1904–1980

Johan Garlepp (John)

Johan Garlepp was born in 1853 in Prussia, He was Charles and Elizabeth's fourth son. When he was 3 years old he emigrated with his family aboard the Electric, in 1856.

John, as he was to become known, grew up on his fathers farm with his brothers.

John had 320 acres in the Lima area from around 1884. Here is a newspaper snippet that I found in The North Eastern Ensign 27 Jun 1884. His brother Herman also had 320 acres in Lima.

In 1889, John married Ellen Agnes Greenwood. Ellen was born in Seymour 6 August, 1864. Tracing her parents has been problematic.

John and Ellen had the following children:

John Garlepp	1891–1922
Eva Agnes Garlepp	1893–1957
Hugh Theodore Garlepp	1896–1957

Thomas Gardner, Gooramgooramgong, 175a

William Wilson, Gowangardie, 107a

James Hogan, pt 24, 25, Gowangardie, 50a

Mary Coffey, pt 24, 25, Gowangardie, 86a—For about 36 acres

Herman Garlepp, Lima, 320a

John Garlepp, Lima, 320a

William A. Higgins, 87, Mokoan, 142a

Joseph Harrison, pt 34, 35, Moorn-

PUBLIC NOTICE.

To Persons Contemplating Building.

JOHN GARLEPP,

Begs to announce that he is prepared to execute all kinds of

CARPENTER'S AND JOINER'S WORK

In 1905 John started advertising his carpentry and joinery work. To the left is an advertisement he inserted into The North Eastern Ensign, 25 August, 1905.

According to an article in the Benalla Standard on 24 October, 1905, John had won a contract for doing some work for the local council.

TENDERS.—Crs. M'Pherson and Kurtzmann met at the Shire-hall yesterday for the purpose of dealing with the tenders received for grubbing and clearing road between John and William Martin, Devenish. Two tenders were received, viz., Patrick Commerford and John Garlepp, and their price was exactly the same, £16. The names were then put in a hat, and Mr. Garlepp's name being drawn out he was given the contract.

LATE TRAIN.—The Yarrawonga train

Benalla Shire Council.

The monthly meeting of the abovenamed was held on Monday last, the following members being present:—Crs Guppy, Smith, Dallas, O'Shanassy, Old, Cook, Cunningham, M'Pherson, Macauley and Kurtzmann.

In the absence of the President Cr Guppy took the chair.

CORRESPONDENCE.

F. G. Wilson wrote stating he had completed the audit of the Shire's accounts and thanked the officers for their assistance.—Received.

A cheque for £579 15s 10d was received from the Treasury, Melbourne, being the council's share of the Endowment of Municipalities for the year ending June, 1905.

The secretaries of Mansfield Hospital, Beechworth Benevolent Asylum, and the Eye and Ear Hospital, Melbourne, wrote asking for the usual donation to their funds. —To be dealt with during the consideration of the Charity vote.

A letter was read from the President of the Charity Carnival, asking for a refund of the £2 10s paid for the use of the Shire hall for a concert given in aid of the Beechworth Benevolent Asylum and the Wangaratta Hospital.—Cr Smith said that the Ladies' Benevolent Society ought to have received part of the sum raised. Cr Kurtzmann: They did very well at Easter, did'nt they? Cr Smith: Yes, but they ought to have been considered, all the same, as they do a good deal of service in the cause of charity. The subject thus ended.

J. Garlepp, Benalla West, wrote stating that he was unable to finish his burning-off contract until after summer and asked that he be allowed £5 for the work done.—The secretary said he had received a letter from Cr Duncan to the effect that ratepayer Martin was complaining about the contractor burning off and that the police were interfering. The Chairman said Martin complained about a tree being felled and set fire to on his land. On the motion of Cr Smith it was agreed to pass £5 subject to the approval of the engineer. In reply to Cr Cook the secretary said the council was not responsible for any damage done by the contractor. The chairman said Martin told him that he (Martin) intended claiming £1 for damage done by fire. Cr Smith: Is that all? The Chairman: Yes. Cr Dallas: Oh; its nothing. The Chairman: Well I know a small patch has been burnt.

In the North Eastern Ensign on Friday 15 December 1905, we find that John couldn't complete some of his burning off contract and asked for a5 pounds for the work done to date.

On 11th January, 1912, John died. Below is the Obituary that was inserted into the North Eastern Ensign on 19 January, 1912.. I have transcribed it, as it's hard to read.

Obituary.

MR J. GARLEPP.

Mr John Garlepp, of Benalla West, expired on the 11th inst., his remains being interred next day in the Church of England portion of the local cemetery, the Rev Mr Farquharson reading the burial service. The late Mr Garlepp was an old resident of the district and spent much of his earlier life at Devenish, where his parents conducted a hotel for some years. He also carried on farming and carpentering at Lima, but sold out at the latter place and about ten years ago settled in Benalla along with his wife and family, the latter consisting of two boys and a girl, the eldest boy being near manhood. Deceased last year partly abandoned his usual calling and took from the council a contract for cleaning the channels of Benalla West, but he had not been long at work before he became ill, and gradually sank till he expired altogether. Deceased was a hard-working man, whose death will be regretted by his many old friends scattered all over the North-east. General sympathy is felt for his wife and family in their bereavement.

Transcription of newspaper article.

Obituary.

Mr J. Garlepp

Mr John Garlepp, of Benalla West, expired on the 11th instance. His remains being interred next day in the Church of England portion of the local cemetery. The Rev Mr Farquharson reading the burial service. The late Mr Garlepp was an old resident of the district and spent much of his earlier life at Devenish, where his parents conducted a hotel for some years. He also carried on farming and carpentering at Lima, but sold out at the latter place and about ten years ago settled in Benalla along with his wife and family, the latter consisting of two boys and a girl, the eldest boy being near manhood. Deceased last year partly abandoned his usual calling and took from the council a contract for cleaning the channels of Benalla West, but he had not been long at work before he became ill and gradually sank till he expired altogether. Deceased was a hard working man, whose death will be regretted by his many old friends scattered all of the North east. General sympathy is felt for his wife and family in their bereavement."

When John died he was 59 years old. His son john was 20 years old, Eva was 19 and Hugh was 16.

On the following page I have included a copy of John's last will and testament.

I have also added copies of the documents used in probate for further information.

"A"   936

This is the Last Will and Testament

made this *thirteenth* day of *December* in the year of our Lord
one thousand nine hundred and *eleven* of *John Garlepp* of
Benalla in the State of *Victoria Carpenter*.

a) Here insert full name and occupation.

J hereby appoint *my wife Ellen Agnes Garlepp*

(b) Here insert the name of person whom you wish to appoint. If a male the word "Executor," female "Executrix," "Company Executor."

(c) Here insert full particulars of bequests.

Executrix of this my Will. **J give devise and bequeath** *all my real*
and personal estate unto my wife Ellen
Agnes Garlepp –

If there is not sufficient room here the matter can be taken over on the next 2 pages, which must be signed by person making will and the witnesses the same as this.

(d) If a male "Testator," female "Testatrix."

Signed by the said Testator and by her declared to be her last Will and Testament in the presence, of us both present at the same time who in her presence at her request and in the presence of each other have hereunto subscribed our names as witnesses.

Signature   *John. Garlepp*

Any person but a beneficiary under the Will can be a witness. An Executor can be a witness.

1st Witness— Name *Lucy C. Carige*
Address *Householder*
Occupation *Benalla*

2nd Witness— Name ____
Address *Bank Manager*
Occupation *Benalla*

Any alterations in the Will must be initialled by the maker and the two witnesses. It is always better to have no alterations if possible, as the same causes extra expense and trouble in obtaining probate after death.

In the Supreme Court of Victoria.
IN THE PROBATE JURISDICTION.

IN THE WILL OF *John Garlepp*
late of *Benalla*
in Victoria *Carpenter* deceased.

BE IT KNOWN that on the *Eighth* day of *February* in the year of our Lord One thousand nine hundred and *twelve* the Will (a true copy whereof is hereunto annexed) of *John Garlepp* late of *Benalla aforesaid Carpenter* deceased, who died on the *eleventh* day of *January* One thousand nine hundred and *twelve* and who had at the

If no Real Estate or no Personal Estate it must be so stated.

time of his death real estate within the jurisdiction sworn not to exceed in value *Two hundred pounds* and personal estate within the jurisdiction sworn not to exceed in value *Thirty pounds ten shillings and five pence* was proved by *Ellen Agnes Garlepp of Benalla aforesaid Widow* the executor named therein, she having been first sworn that she would well and truly collect and administer according to law the estate of the said

deceased, and would exhibit and deposit in the office of the Master-in-Equity a true and perfect inventory of the said estate within three months of the order granting probate and a true and just account of her administration of the said estate within fifteen months of the said order.

Given at Melbourne this *Twentieth* day of *February* in the year of our Lord One thousand nine hundred and *twelve*.

J. Carter.
Registrar of Probates.

DN
13/2/12

5430.

(1) And codicil or
codicils, if any.

IN THE WILL [1] of *John Garlepp*

late of *Benalla*

in Victoria, *Carpenter* deceased.

I *Ellen Agnes Garlepp*
of *Benalla* in Victoria,

Widow make oath and say—

1. That *I am* seeking to obtain Probate of the Will [1] ——— of the above-named *John Garlepp* deceased, and that I am a person of the full age of 21 years.

2. The said deceased died on the *eleventh* day of *January* One thousand nine hundred and *twelve* and was at the time of *his* death *married*

(2) If any codicils, state the number and date of each.

(3) Or are where codicils.

(4) Insert full christian and surname and residence of each executor.

3. The said deceased left a Will [2] ——— bearing date the *13*[th] day of *December* One thousand nine hundred and *eleven* which is as *I* believe the last Will and Testament of the said deceased. and which is [3] ——— unrevoked.

4. By *his* said Will the testator appointed *me Ellen Agnes Garlepp of Benalla* executrix thereof. At the time the said Will was executed Testator was a person of the full age of 21 years.

(5) If codicils, they must also be marked.

(6) Insert full christian and surname and residence of each of the subscribing witnesses to the Will.

(7) If no real estate or no personal property insert but did not leave any real estate (or personal property, as the case may be)

5. The paper writing hereunto annexed marked "A" is the true last Will and Testament of the said deceased as *I* verily believe. [5]

6. The said Will was executed in the presence of [6] *Lucy Chalmers Carige of Benalla in Victoria Nauschoider and Edwin Fitzroy Lusignan of Benalla in Victoria Bank Manager and both of us then present Resident at 13 Benalla*

7. The said deceased left property in Victoria not exceeding in value the sum of [7] *two hundred and thirty pounds ten shillings and fifteen pence* consisting of real estate of the value of £ *200 . 0 . 0* ———— and personal estate of the value of £ *30 . 10 . 5* Particulars of which said real and personal estate are set out in the statement filed herewith, *and marked B*

8. That if *I* obtain Probate *I* will well and truly collect and administer according to law to the best of *my* knowledge and ability the property lands and hereditaments goods chattels and credits of the said deceased at the time of *his* death which at any time after shall come to the power or control hands or possession of *me* as *his* executrix or of any other person or persons for *me* that *I* will make or cause to be made a true and perfect inventory of all and singular the property lands and hereditaments goods chattels and credits of the said deceased which shall have come to the hands possession or knowledge of *me* or to the hands or possession of any other person or persons for *me* and the same so made will sign with *my* proper handwriting and will exhibit and deposit or cause to be exhibited and deposited the same inventory in the office of the Master-in-Equity within three calendar months next ensuing the order granting probate ; and, further, that *I* will make or cause to be made a true and just account of the administration of the estate which *I* have undertaken as to *my* receipts and disbursements and as to what portion is retained by *me* and what portion remains uncollected. and the same so made will sign with *my* proper handwriting and will exhibit and deposit or cause to be exhibited and deposited the same account in the said office of the Master-in-Equity within fifteen calendar months next ensuing the order granting Probate.

9. That to the best of my knowledge, information, and belief, the said deceased did not within the space of two years preceding the date of *his* death convey or otherwise dispose of, for other than adequate valuable consideration, any real or personal property of which he was seised or possessed.

Sworn at *Benalla* in the State
of Victoria, this *Seventeenth* day of
January One thousand nine
hundred and *twelve* .
Before me,

E A Garlepp

Adolph Fox
Registrar of the County Court.
A Commissioner of the Supreme Court for taking Affidavits.

In the Supreme Court

OF VICTORIA.

PROBATE JURISDICTION.

IN THE Will of John Garlepp
late of Benalla in the State of Victoria, Carpenter
deceased

This is the paper writing marked "*" referred to in the annexed Affidavit of Ellen Agnes Garlepp
Sworn this 17th day of January 1912
Before me Joseph Fox
A Commissioner of the Supreme Court of Victoria for taking Affidavits.
A Registrar of County Courts.

STATEMENT OF ASSETS AND LIABILITIES.

ASSETS.	£	s	d	LIABILITIES.	£	s	d
REAL ESTATE.							
About a quarter acre of freehold land situate in Garden Street Benalla on which is erected an eight roomed weather-board dwelling house and which is fenced with a picket fence the capital value of which as assessed by the Municipality of the Shire of Benalla, is two hundred pounds.	200	0	0	N. Moodie of Benalla Merchant. Goods	2	7	5
PERSONAL ESTATE.							
Landed Property held under Lease or Licence from the Crown	Nil						
Rents	Nil						
Crops	Nil						
Live Stock [1]	Nil						
Farming Implements [2]	Nil						
Carriages, &c. [2]	Nil						
Harness and Saddlery	Nil						
Furniture [3]	10						
Watches, Trinkets, Jewellery, &c. [4] Old Silver Watch	1	0	0				
Money in Hand or House	12						
Money in Bank [5]	Nil						
Current Account [5]	Nil						
Money in Bank, on Deposit [5]	Nil						
Interest	Nil						
Debentures	Nil						
Mortgages	Nil						
Mortgages Interest	Nil						
Life Policies [6]	Nil						
Bonus	Nil						
Shares	Nil						
Dividends	Nil						
Plant, &c.	Nil						
Tools	5						
Debts due to the Estate	2	10	5				
Stock in a Shop or Business	Nil			Balance for Duty	228	3	0
Goodwill	Nil						
Interest in a Deceased Person's Estate	Nil						
	230	**10**	**5**		**2**	**7**	**5**

[1] State number and value of each.
[2] Specify and give separate values.
[3] If over £50 a list is required.
[4] Specify and give separate values.
[5] Name of Bank must be given.
[6] Name of Society must be given.

In the foregoing prescribed form of statement the assets in the personal estate must in set down under the heads above set out. In any case in which no assets exist corresponding to any one of the said headings, such heading must nevertheless be set down with the word "Nil" against it. If there are any assets not coming properly under any of the said headings, such assets must be included in the said statement under a special heading describing the same.

I certify the total net value of this estate, in and out of Victoria, does not exceed £2,000, and the final balance of this estate to be £ and the amount chargeable with duty to be £ at one-half of the percentage fixed by Part II. of the First Schedule to the *Administration and Probate Act 1903.*

Officer to assess Duty.

On 15 January, 1913 there was an article in the Age newspaper that reports of an act of cruelty to a dog, by John junior.

Below is a copy of the article that appeared in the Benalla Standard on Friday 17 January 1913

I have transcribed this article on the following pages.

CRUELTY TO A DOG.
BENALLA, Tuesday.

Before Mr. Beaven, at the local court to-day, John Garlepp was charged with maliciously wounding a staghound, the property of Charles Turnbull. The Society for the Prevention of Cruelty to Animals prosecuted.

The evidence disclosed that defendant, with his sister, was out in a paddock shooting, and from a distance of about five yards shot the dog in the neck, making a wound three inches long, and then shot him in the hind quarters. Subsequently, over twenty pellets were taken out of the dog's hind quarters.

The defence was that the dog followed Garlepp, who tried to send it home, and then, to frighten it, discharged two barrels in its direction.

Mr. Beaven made an order for the payment of £4 damages, and fined defendant £5, in default three months' hard labor. Defendant was allowed seven days in which to pay the fine.

SHOOTING A DOG
FINE, £5; DAMAGE, £4.

A case in which a great deal of interest was taken was heard at the Benalla court on Tuesday, before Mr. J. W. W. Beaven, P.M., when Constable Woods charged John Garlepp that on November 28 he did unlawfully and maliciously wound a dog—a staghound—the property of one, Charles Turnbull. Mr. F. T. Brown appeared for the Society for the Prevention of Cruelty to Animals to assist the prosecution, and Mr. Q. H. Pyne for the defendant, who pleaded not guilty.

Mr. Brown, in opening the case, said the dog in question was a valuable one. On November 29 the dog was found to be in a bad condition, having been shot in the neck and hind quarters at close range. They thought the case too serious to be brought under the Prevention of Cruelty to Animals Act, and so had charged defendant under section 212 of the Crimes Act.

Charles Turnbull, auctioneer, said he resided in Garden-street, and defendant lived next door. Defendant would have seen the dog about his premises. On the morning of the 28th or 29th November he found the dog very badly wounded. He was shot in the neck and also in the back, the hind leg being paralysed. About 20 grains of No. 2 shot were taken from the neck, and the shot must have been discharged at short range.

To Mr. Pyne: The dog was still bad and he did not think it would ever get better. There was a wound about three inches in extent in the neck.

To Mr. Brown: The dog was a favorite with the family.

To the P.M.: The dog was now paralysed. He was worth nothing for hunting now. Could not have bought the dog for £5.

Adelaide C. Bowden, residing at the Royal farm, said when going home about 7 p.m. on November 28 she saw Jack and Eva Garlepp in Smith's paddock. They had two dogs with them, and Jack Garlepp, who had a gun with him, shot the brown dog, who jumped about. Garlepp then ran about a dozen yards and shot the dog again in the hind quarters. He then ran behind a tree. She had seen the dog several times.

To Mr. Pyne: She was at the Royal farm gate, and was about 50 or 60 yards away from Garlepp. Knew the Garlepp's by sight. She would say the dog was about five yards away from Garlepp. She did not measure the distance, but that was the distance as it appeared to her from where she was standing. Garlepp's had their own dog with them too. After the second shot the dog fell down. She went on to the Royal farm and did not trouble any more about the dog. Thought they were going to kill it outright. She told Mrs. Lahrs, when she got to the farm, what she had seen.

To Mr. Beaven: Supposed when defendant ran behind the tree he was frightened the dog might bite him.

Eva Garlepp was called, but wanted her expenses, and was asked to step down.

Constable Woods said he saw Garlepp in Arundel-street. He said he was out the previous Thursday with his sister, shooting rabbits. Accused denied having shot a dog, and said it would be a lie if anybody said he did. He went and saw Eva Garlepp, and then saw Garlepp again, when he said to him. "I have a signed statement here from your sister that you did shoot the dog." Garlepp then said that he did shoot the dog. He said the dog would follow him, and he wanted to send the dog back.

To Mr. Pyne: He said that the dog would not go back.

That was the case.

Mr. Pyne said that the dog would follow these people, and accused simply fired at the dog with the intention of sending it home. According to his information the dog was 50 or 60 yards away, and the shot was fired in the direction of the dog, but with no intention of hurting it. Garlepp had tried to get the dog to go back before that.

Eva Garlepp, sister of defendant, said at the end of November she was with her brother, out shooting rabbits in Smith's paddock. She was close enough to him to see what he was going to do. Mr. Turnbull's dog was following her brother. She was only there when he fired at it to frighten it away. The dog at the time was not very far away. It was about 4½ yards away from him.

was not very far away. It was about 4½ yards away from him.

Mr. Pyne: Are you sure?

Mr. Brown: Well, I know it is very annoying.

The witness then left the box.

The defendant made a statement in which he said the dog was following him. He tried several times to chase him back, but he would not go. He then fired a couple of shots in the dog's direction, and it ran away. He then went on.

Both Mr. Pyne and Mr. Brown said they would like to ask a question, but the P.M. refused to allow such a thing.

The P.M.: What is the defendant?

Mr. Brown: He did have the contract for cleaning the gutters, but now he does nothing. He is a laborer.

The P.M.: He wants imprisonment, with hard labor.

Mr. Pyne pointed out that the boy was the eldest son of his mother, who was a widower. He was the support of a large family.

The P.M.: This poor animal should not suffer on account of that. The defendant will be ordered to pay £4 damages, which I assess at that, and a fine of £5, in default, three month's imprisonment, with hard labor.

Mr. Pyne said they hoped to be able to find the money, but he asked for a week's time.

Seven days was allowed in which to pay the fine, which has since been paid.

SHOOTING A DOG

FINE, £5; DAMAGE, £4.

A case in which a great deal of interest was taken was hoard at the Benalla court on Tuesday, before Mr. J. W. W. Beaven, P.M., when Constable Woods charged John Garlepp that on November 28 he did unlawfully and maliciously wound a dog - a staghound - the property of one Charles Turnbull.

Mr F. T. Brown appeared for the Society for the Prevention of Cruelty to Animals to assist the prosecution, and Mr Q. H. Pyne for the defendant, who pleaded not guilty.

Mr. Brown, in opening the case, said the dog in question was a valuable one. On November 29 the dog was found to be in a bad condition, having been shot in the neck and hind quarters at close range. They thought the case too serious to be brought under the Prevention of Cruelty to Animals Act, and so had charged defendant under section 212 of the Crimes Act.

Charles Turnbull, auctioneer, said he resided in Garden Street, and defendant lived next door. Defendant would have seen the dog about his premises. On the morning of the 28th or 29th November he found the dog very badly wounded. He was shot in the neck and also in the back, the hind leg being paralysed.

About 20 grains of No 2 shot were taken from the neck, and the shot must have been discharged at short range.

To Mr. Pyne: The dog was still bad and he did not think it would ever got better. There was a wound about three inches in extent in the neck.

To Mr. Brown; The dog was a favorite with the family.

To the P M. : The dog was now paralysed. He was worth nothing for hunting now.. Could not have bought the dog for £5.

Adelaide C. Bowden, residing at the Royal farm, said when going home about 7 p.m. on November 28 she saw Jack and Eva Garlepp in Smith's paddock. They had two dogs with them, and Jack Garlepp who had a gun with him, shot the brown dog, who jumped about. Garlepp then ran about a dozen yards and shot the dog again in the hind quarters. He then ran behind a tree. She had seen the dog several times.

To Mr. Pyne: She was at the Royal farm gate, and was about 50 or 60 yards away from Garlepp. Knew the Garlepp's by sight. She would say the dog was about five yards away from Garlepp. She did not measure the distance, but that was the distance as it appeared to her from where she was standing.

Garlepp's had their own dog with them too. After the second shot the dog fell down. She went on to the Royal farm and did not ! trouble any more about the dog. Thought they were going to kill it outright. she told Mrs. Luhrs, when she got to the farm, what she had seen.

To. Mr. Beaven: Supposed when defendant ran behind the tree he was frightened the dog might bite him.

Eva Garlepp was called, but wanted her expenses, and was asked to step down,

Constable Woods said he saw Garlepp in Arundel street. He said he was out the previous Thursday with his sister, shooting rabbits. Accused denied having shot a dog, and said it would be a lie if anybody said he did. He went and saw Eva Garlepp, and then saw Garlepp again, when he said to him. 'I have a signed statement, here from your sister that you did shoot the dog,' Garlepp then said that he did shoot the dog. He said the dog would follow him, and he wanted to send the dog back.

To Mr. Pyne: He said that the dog would not go back. That was the case. Mr. Pyne said that the dog would follow these people, and accused simply fired at the dog with the intention of sending it home. According to his information the dog was 50 or 60 yards away, and the shot was fired in the direction of the dog, but with no intention of hurting it. Garlepp had tried to get the dog to go back before that.

Eva Garlepp, sister of defendant, said at the end of November she was with her brother, out shooting rabbits in Smith's paddock She was close enough to him to see what he was going to do. Mr. Turnbull's dog was

following her brother. She was only there when he fired at it to frighten It away. The dog at the time was not very far away. It was about 4 1/2 yards away from him.

Mr. Pyne: Are you sure?

Mr. Brown : Well. I know it is very annoying. The witness then left the box..

The defendant made a statement in which he said the dog was following him. He tried several times to chase him back, but he would not go. He then fired a couple of shots in the dog's direction, and it ran away. He then went on.

Both Mr. .Pyne and Mr. Brown said they would like to ask a question, but the P.M. refused to allow such a thing.

The P.M.: What is the defendant?

Mr. Brown: He did have the contract for cleaning the gutters, but now he does nothing. -He is a laborer.

The P.M.: He wants imprisonment, with hard labor.

Mr. Pyne pointed out that the boy was the eldest son of his mother, who was a widower. He was the support of a large family.

The P.M. : This poor animal should not suffer on account of that. The defendant will be ordered to pay £4 damages, which I assess at that, and a fine of £5, in default, three mouth's imprisonment-, with hard labor.

Mr. Pyne said they hoped to be able to find the money, but he asked for a week's time. Seven days with fine, which has since been paid as allowed in which to pay

Mr. Pyne said they hoped to be able to find the money, but he asked for » week's time. Seven days was allowed iy which to pay the fine, which has since been paid.

> On 16 September, 1920, Eva appeared in court. The charge said the following:
>
> *"Defendant at Benalla being a common prostitute did importune a person in a public place towit Bridge St."*
>
> The case was remanded until October with a 10 pound bail set. It was again remanded until November.
>
> The case was dismissed in November.

In 1921, the electoral rolls are showing Ellen, her son John and daughter Eva are still Living in Garden Street, Benalla. John is working as a labourer. He seems to be the main support for the family.

There is a birth and death registered of a child called Albert John Garlipp, with mother Eva Garlipp in 1921 in Fitzroy. I suspect this child belonged to our Eva, and that she stayed with family to have the child who unfortunately died.

On 6 May 1921, John junior was in an accident. The article below , which appeared in the Benalla Standard 10 May, 1921 explains what happened.

are required not in the cities but in in the country districts. It is to be hoped that there will be eliminated from this new policy of the Government any suspicion of party feeling but that all will join in making a great effort to insure its being a success.

PROBATE.—The will has been lodged for probate of Bessie Blackburne, late of Ryan's Creek, married woman. who left personal estate valued at £1299 8/9 to her sons. Her son, Robert Blackburne, is appointed executor. Messrs. F T. Brown and Sons are proctors to the estate.

UNIVERSAL HALF - HOLIDAY. — At a round table conference at Wagga between the Shopkeepers' Association and the Wagga Eight Hours' Association a proposal was discussed for making a general half-holiday on Saturday, in lieu of the present arrangement, under which stores close on Wednesday afternoon and remain open on Saturday until 9 o'clock. It was unanimously resolved to obtain signatures to a joint petition signed by shopkeepers and employees, to be presented to the Minister, praying that legislation be introduced next session to provide for Saturday as a universal half holiday in New South Wales.

ACCIDENT WITH MANGLE —On Friday last Miss Henderson, who is employed at the Benalla hotel, met with a very painful accident while putting some sheets through the mangle. The sheets slipped, with the result that Miss Henderson's second and third fingers of the left hand were drawn in between the rollers and were crushed. The aid of a medical man was obtained, and he dressed the fingers.

SERIOUS ACCIDENT.—On Saturday morning a very serious accident happened to Mr. John Garlepp, of Benalla West, who was temporarily employed by the shire council. With Mr. W. Burns, Mr Garlepp was engaged in carting loam from a pit on the river bank to the north of the enclosure to the oval, where it was being spread. While loading the dray in the pit Mr. Garlepp had his back to the face of the cut, when his mate observed that

of the cut, when his mate observed that the earth above was sliding. He called out "Look out!" to Mr. Garlepp, but unfortunately the warning was too late, and from two to three tons of earth fell on and buried Mr. Garlepp. Mr. Burns called for assistance, and Mr. Briggs, the caretaker of the Gardens, and others were quickly on the spot and removed the earth from the buried man. They then found that he was unable to move his legs, and a doctor, who shortly afterwards arrived, found that the spine was seriously injured and both legs paralysed. The case was regarded as very serious, and an ambulance was procured from the railway station and the injured man was conveyed to the Wangaratta Hospital by the midday train. Reports received from the hospital confirm the view as to the seriousness of the injuries. Much sympathy has been expressed for Mr. Garlepp, who was a general favorite, and has always been known as a most painstaking workman.

BUSINESS CHANGE.—Mr. A. M'Nicholson has disposed of his butchering business in Bridge street to Mr. J. L. Birmingham, of Shepparton, who arrived in Benalla from that town on Thursday last. Our Shepparton contemporary, the "Advertiser," says that Mr. Birmingham was very popular in that town.

GAZETTE NOTICES.—The following notices appeared in last week's issue of the "Government Gazette"; —License to occupy unused road: M. E. Lester, Dueran, 60 acres, Dueran and Barwite. Land available: 397 acres, Whitfield, 3rd class land.

The Benalla Standard gave an update to John's situation on 13 May, 1921. (right). And on 17 May, 1921 (below)

THE ACCIDENT TO MR. GARLEPP.—In reference to the accident which happened to Mr. John Garlepp, of Benalla, on Saturday morning last, when he arrived at the Wangaratta Hospital and an examination was made as to his injuries it was found that his back was broken. Since his arrival at the institution named he has been making fair progress and is getting on as well as can be expected considering the very severe injuries he received.

THE ACCIDENT IN THE GARDENS

At yesterday's meeting of the Benalla Shire Council the President (Cr. Walker) reported on the accident to Mr. John Garlepp while engaged by the council, and said that at the Wangaratta Hospital the X rays was not nearly strong enough, and there was no spine expert there. He, with Mr. Knox, arranged for Mr. Garlepp to be taken to Melbourne, where a much stronger machine would be obtained. Five doctors examined him, and that night they would know what the extent of the injuries were. There was no chance of saving his life at Wangaratta, so they thought they should shift him to Melbourne to give him a chance.

The action of the president and secretary was approved.

Cr. Cook asked if the council was covered with insurance.

The President: Yes.

Cr. Cook said that when Mr. Lawford gave the plant he gave the hospital management a free hand.

The President said that was so, but the machines at other hospitals in Melbourne were not strong enough. That at the Melbourne Hospital was ten times as strong as general machines.

The North Easter Ensign, also covered the story on 20 May 1921 (below)

The young man (John Garlepp) referred to in last issue of the Ension as having sustained a serious accident by a fall of earth upon him whilst digging out sand along the Broken River, and who was subsequently railed to the Wangaratta Hospital, was sent some days ago to a metropolitan institution for inspection under the X rays. The latest account to hand respecting him shows the spine has been seriously damaged and it is questionable whether he will be ever able to work again. Nevertheless, the unfortunate young man is in good spirits, though some of his friends think he will not survive

Transcription of the above article is below.

"The young man (John Garlepp) referred to in last issue of the Ensign as having sustained a serious accident by a fall of earth upon him whilst digging out sand along the Broken River, and who was subsequently railed to the Wangaratta Hospital, was sent some days ago to a metropolitan institution for inspection under the X rays. The latest account to hand respecting him shows the spine has been seriously damaged and it is questionable whether he will ever be able to work again. Nevertheless, the unfortunate young man is in good spirits, though some of his friends think he will not survive."

cai man.

THE ACCIDENT TO MR JOHN GARLEPP.—During last week end Mr. Geo Walker, the shire president, received word from the authorities of the Melbourne Hospital to the effect that the injuries which Mr. Garlepp had sustained in the accident in the Benalla gardens last Saturday fortnight had been examined through the X rays, and the report of the medical men was, his friends will regret to hear, of a very unfavorable character. We understand that an effort is to be made to have him transferred to the Austin Hospital for Incurables.

John died 26 January, 1922. The Benalla Standard wrote an obituary and published it 27 January, 1922. (right)

The North Eastern Ensign wrote the following on 3 February, 1922

MR JOHN GARLEPP

At the Melbourne Hospital at 6 30 last Thursday morning there passed away Mr John Garlepp, who, it will be remembered, sustained very severe injuries as the result of an accident sustained last April by a fall of earth whilst engaged in an excavation near the river bank procuring some filling for depressions in the local oval, preparing for the football season. First of all he was removed to the Wangaratta Hospital, but the spinal injuries he had received were of such a nature that it was thought advisable to remove him to the city for special treatment, although very little hope of his recovery was held out from the start. Deceased, who was a very popular young man, was unmarried, but leaves a widowed mother, a sister and a brother. The body was brought to Benalla for interment.

The next update we have, was found in the Benalla Standard on 24 May, 1921. (left)

OBITUARY

MR JOHN GARLEPP

It is with extreme regret we record the death of Mr John Garlepp, the sad event taking place at the Melbourne Hospital at 6.30 yesterday morning. It will be remembered that last April Mr. Garlepp was assisting in filling up the oval in the Gardens with earth to prepare for the football season. When excavating near the river bank a large quantity of earth fell on him and caused an injury to his spine, and at the time it was recognised that although he might linger for a considerable time, there would be no recovery. He was removed to the Wangaratta Hospital, but as it was thought he would have a better chance in Melbourne, he was taken to the Melbourne hospital, where he has had the most careful attention; but, unfortunately nothing could be done for him. His limbs have been paraylsed ever since, but he has retained his senses and continued cheerful. On Monday morning he was seized with an attack of vomiting, and it was feared the end had come. However, he rallied, and on Tuesday appeared as well as usual. The end came yesterday, however, as stated. Deceased was a very popular young fellow, and deep regret will be felt at his untimely death. He was unmarried, but leaves a widowed mother, sister and brother. His mother and sister left for Melbourne yesterday morning.

The body will be brought to Benalla this morning for interment in the local cemetery. The funeral will leave his late residence at 4 p.m.

The Argus newspaper, on 17 February, 1922 wrote the following article. I have transcribed it because it is a little hard to read.

CRUSHED BY A FALL OF EARTH.

At the Morgue yesterday, the coroner (Dr. Cole) held an inquiry concerning the death of John Jones Garlepp, a labourer, 30 years of age, of Garden street, West Benalla, who was crushed by a fall of earth while removing debris from a pit at Benalla.

Garlepp and another man were at work when the fall took place. It completely buried Garlepp. His fellow-workmen dug him out, and he was taken to Wangaratta Hospital by train, and subsequently to Melbourne Hospital, where he died on January 26.

A finding that death was due to fracture of the spine accidentally caused at Benalla on May 18 last was recorded.

THE LATE MR. JOHN GARLEPP.—On Thursday last an inquest was held at the Melbourne morgue concerning the death of Mr. John Garlepp, which took place in the Melbourne Hospital recently as the result of an accident near the Benalla Gardens on 7th May last, when a quantity of earth fell on him and injured his spine. After hearing the evidence of the curator of the gardens (Mr. H. Briggs) and Mr. George Burns, who were working with deceased at the time, Dr. Cole, the coroner, returned a verdict of accidental death, there being no blame attachable to any one.

On 6 June, 1922, the Benalla Standard reported (article on the right) that 100 pounds was paid for Workers Compensation.

"*CRUSHED BY A FALL OF EARTH*

At the Morgue yesterday, the coroner (Dr Cole) held an inquiry concerning the death of John Jones Garlepp, a labourer, 30 years of age of Garden Street, West Benalla, who was crushed by a fall of earth while removing debris from a pit at Benalla.

Garlepp and another man were at work when the fall took place. It completely buried Garlepp. His fellow workmen dug him out, and he was taken to Wangaratta Hospital by train and subsequently to Melbourne Hospital where he died on January 26.

In finding that death was due to fracture of the spine accidentally caused at Benalla on May 18 1921 was recorded. "

The article to the left was in the Benalla
Standard 21st February, 1922.

COUNTY COURT.—The sittings of the Benalla County Court are fixed to take place to-morrow, when His Honor Judge Dethridge will preside. The list of cases is as follows:—Application for an order allocating amounts paid into court as compensation under the Workers Compensation Act re the late Hartley William Mitchell; George May v. H. G. Woodham, claim for £146 18/9, work and labor done and hire of chattels; Maher v. Haurabam, claim for £72, half commission on sale of property; D. J. M'Lelland v. R. Jones, goods sold and delivered, £39; F. Fraser v. M'Cormick, claim for £223 for wages due under an agreement. Application for an order for the disposal and and investment under the Workers Compensation Act of £100 paid into court in respect to the death of the late John Garlepp.

Benalla Standard (Vic. : 1901 - 1940) / Tue 11 Apr 1922

sion.—Attended to.
From State Accident Association office, asking that a meeting be arranged for a conference with Mrs. Garlepp and Rev. N. D. Herring and the shire secretary, for Wednesday morning, (15th March,) at 11.30, to discuss matters with their inspector re J. J. Garlepp, deceased, and forwarding forms for completion to be handed to the Registrar of the County Court.—Left in Mr. Knox's hands.
From J. H. Croucher, applying to purchase unused road containing about 2¼ acres, between his property (33e) and Woods Bros. (33a).—Sale to be opposed, but no objection to the lease.

There is very little information about Hugh. He didn't marry. On 2 September 1926 he found his way into the news. The Benalla Standard reported on 7 September, 1926 that Hugh had a brush with death. I have transcribed it for easier reading.

A Narrow Escape.—A miraculous escape from death was experienced by a young man named Hugh Garlepp on Thursday last. In company with another young man named Plant, he was out rabbit shooting with a pea-rifle. By some means the rifle slipped from his hand, and in falling struck the ground with the stock. The concussion caused the charge to explode, the bullet taking an upward course, cutting a scar along Garlepp's cheek, grazing the temple, and passing through the inside lining of his hat. The wound bled profusely, and Garlepp was brought to Benalla for treatment, two stitches being necessary. Besides leaving an ugly wound, no serious results are anticipated, but another quarter of an inch would have meant instant death.

"A Narrow Escape.— A miraculous escape from death was experienced by a young man named Hugh Garlepp on Thursday last. In company with another young man named Plant, he was out rabbit shooting with a pea rifle. By some means the rifle slipped from his hand and in falling struck the ground with the stock. The concussion caused the charge to explode, the bullet taking an upward course, cutting a scar along Garlepp's cheek, grazing the temple, and passing through the inside lining of his hat. The would bled profusely, and Garlepp was brought to Benalla for treatment, two stitches being necessary. Besides leaving an ugly wound, no serious results are anticipated, but another quarter of an inch would have meant instant death. "

I found another article about Hugh in the Benalla Standard on 23 October, 1934.

A champion bike rider…. That's a good news story.

BENALLA CYCLE CLUB

GARLEPP WINS 20 MILE RACE

The Benalla Cycle Club held a 20-mile road race on Saturday, being the last race for the two cups. With T. Glazebrook, J. Cleary, A. M'Millan and A. Rodler back again after a spell, the race was full of interest. The winner turned up in H. Garlepp, who off the limit rode a good race, to win, with R. Fox second and T. White a close third. Fastest time went to T. Glazebrook. W. White won the "New Star" cup and E. Brennan the Road Season Cup.

On Saturday week the club will hold the last race of the road season with a 5-mile race, when riders from Shepparton and Wangaratta will take part. Mr. Murphy, manager of the Farmers Arms Hotel for Mrs. Richards, has given the club the first prize of £3, so the boys are looking forward to a good day.

To make ends meet Ellen seems to have rented out her house. She ran into some trouble and it seems from an article in the North Eastern Ensign on 13 August, 1926, Ellen had applied to have him ejected from her house. I have transcribed this below:

Ejectment Order.

GRANTED BY COURT

"Ejectment Order. GRANTED BY COURT. Ellen Agnes Garlepp of Benalla West, applied at the local court on Tuesday for an order to eject Edward Dodemaid from tenement in Garden st Benalla West The bench was occupied by messers G.Walker and H.Guppy J's.P. Mr R. P. Lewers appeared for the complaint there being no appearance from the defendant In setting out this case Mr Lewers that it was one of unusual character. It was brought under the Land and Tenancy Act combined with the' Justices' Act. Complainant had let the house to Dodemaide on a weekly tenancy she could not get any rent. She served a notice to quit on him. He eventually left and took the key with him. She now sought for an order from the court. Michael Harnatty senior constable of police at Benalla said that he served an owner's notice to recover possession on defendant on 24th July. He read it and explained it to him. To the bench - he was in the premises at the time and said he would got out. I believe he did leave a few days afterwards. Ellen Agnes Gerlepp. the complainant, stated that defendant rented the house at 6/- per week. She could not get him out so she served him with a notice. He left left Saturday and took the key. The Bench thereupon made the necessary ejectment to take effect within seven days.

Ejectment Order.

GRANTED BY COURT

Ellen Agnes Garlepp, of Benalla West applied at the local court on Tuesday for an order to eject Edward Dodemaide from tenement in Garden-street, Benalla West.

The bench was occupied by Messrs G. Walker and H. Guppy, J's.P.

Mr R. P. Lewers appeared for the complainant, there being no appearance of the defendant.

In setting out this case, Mr Lewers stated that it was one of unusual character. It was brought under the Land and Tenancy Act combined with the Justices' Act. Complainant had let the house to Dodemaide on a weekly tenancy She could not get any rent. She served a notice to quit on him. He eventually left and took the key with him. She now sought for an order from the court.

Michael Harnatty, senior-constable of police at Benalla, said that he served an owner's notice to recover possession on defendant on 24th July. He read it and explained it to him.

To the Bench—He was in the premises at the time, and he would get out. I believe he did leave a few days afterwards.

Ellen Agnes Gerlepp, the complainant, stated that defendant rented the house at 6/- per week. She could not get him out, so she served him with a notice. He left last Saturday and took the key.

The Bench thereupon made the necessary ejectment to take effect within seven days.

Ellen Agnes died in September, 1927. The below articles were found in the Benalla Standard and the North Eastern Ensign on 23 September, 1927

MRS. ELLEN AGNES GARLEPP

On Tuesday evening, Mr. Hughie Garlepp, had occasion to go to his mother's room at their residence, Garden street, Benalla West, and upon speaking to her received no reply. Upon examination he found life to be extinct. The deceased lady was borne at Seymour 63 years ago, and some 24 years later married at Benalla, her husband having predeceased her. For some years she has been ailing, and her death was not altogether unexpected, even though it happened suddenly. She leaves grown up family of a son and daughter (Hughie Theodore and Eva Agnes). The remains were interred in the Benalla cemetery yesterday Canon Herring conducting the burial service, and Mr. E. A. Abbott had charge of the funeral arrangements

MRS. ELLEN A. GARLEPP.

The death occurred on Tuesday evening last of Mrs. Ellen Agnes Garlepp, relict of the late John Garlepp. Deceased had not enjoyed good health of late years, and she passed away very suddenly on the evening stated. The late Mrs. Garlepp was a native of Seymour. She married at Benalla at the age of 24 years, and since that time she has resided here. She reared a family of two sons, John (deceased) and Hughie Theodore, and one daughter, Eva Agnes, for whom deep sympathy is felt in their bereavement. The remains were interred in the Benalla cemetery on Thursday. Canon Herring officiating at the graveside.

Nothing more is known about Eva apart from her death in 1957 in Cobram. Her death is registered as Eva Agnes Thompson. In 1937 she is living at 12 Garden Street Benalla, but there is no husband living there with her. I'm not sure if she was married and it was never registered, or if she has assumed a partners name, or just changed her name for her own reasons. I have no further information about her.

At some time around 1950, Hugh moves into the Ovens Benevolent Asylum. He is around 55 years old.

Hugh died 24 August, 1957 while he was an inmate at the Asylum.

Here is a short history of The Ovens Benevolent Asylum history:

1856 - 1860   The service came into being as a result of the amalgamation of two of the oldest hospitals in north-eastern Victoria and the inclusion of part of a third hospital, Mayday Hills. Initially, the Ovens District Hospital (Ovens Goldfields Hospital) was established to meet the acute health needs of the thriving mining town of Beechworth in 1856.

Originally located in Church Street, it was the only hospital located between Melbourne and Goulburn, NSW. In 1940 it relocated to the current Sydney Road site.

1861 - 1934   The establishment of the Ovens Benevolent Asylum on Warner Road was first mooted in 1861, when on the 22nd July a public meeting was held with the object of building a district Benevolent Asylum. The function of this Asylum was to provide accommodation and care for gold miners who were permanently injured, and for women and children who were penniless, homeless, or whose parents were guests of the State.

1935 - 2001   In 1935, the name of the Benevolent Asylum was changed to Ovens Benevolent Home. In February 1973 the name was changed to Ovens Hospital for the Aged and in October 1974 the name was changed again, this time to Ovens and Murray Hospital for the Aged. On 17th August 1992 The Beechworth Hospital was formed as a result of the amalgamation of the Ovens District Hospital and the Ovens and Murray Hospital for the Aged.

OVENS BENEVOLENT ASYLUM.

Beechworth, Victoria

Credit: Ovens benevolent asylum and grounds, Beechworth, Victoria (Australia). Process print. Wellcome Collection. Source: Wellcome Collection.

Wilhelm Garlepp (William)

Wilhelm was born in February, 1856 in Prussia. He was the 5th son of Carl and Elizabeth Garlepp.

Wilhelm was only about 6 months old when his parents boarded the Electric with his older brothers in August, 1856 to emigrate to Australia.

When William, as he had become known, was about 29, he married **Sarah Ann French.** Sarah had a daughter in 1884,

Mary Agnes French   1884-1951

The registration doesn't list a father, however, she may have been Williams, as he married Sarah the following year.

Sarah was the 5th of 8 siblings born to John French (1833-1917) and Ellen O'Halloran (1833-1903)

John French had arrived in Australia aboard the Pola in 1853. He had emigrated from Lancashire, England. And landed in Port Phillip, Victoria.

Ellen arrived in Australia aboard the China in 1854. She came from Clare, Ireland with two of her sisters, Mary and Bridget. They landed in Sydney.

John and Ellen met, and later married on 2 April, 1855 in St Mary's Church, Sydney. The couple lived around New South Wales and Sarah was born in Wagga Wagga.

Two of Sarah's sisters married Garlepp brothers. Ellen married Ernest in 1884. And Catherine, married Henry in 1886.

I will write a book about the French family. So keep a look out for it.

William and Sarah lived in Violet Town, Victoria, where they had a daughter,

Elizabeth Anistasia Garlepp   1886-1886   died at 7 months of age.

The family then moved to South Melbourne. Where they had the following children.

William George Garlepp   1887–1964
Ernest Garlepp   1891–(No death registered)

In 1892 William was charged under warrant with deserting his children and remanded to Port Melbourne gaol.

He must have gone back home, because two more children are born:
Sarah Ann Garlepp   1893–1980
Violet Lily Myrtle Garlepp   1898–

In 1896 William is living at 111 Thistlethwaite Street, South Melbourne, where he was working as labourer.

We unfortunately do not hear any more about William. There is no death registered. I think he may have changed his name.

Sarah went on to marry again. I cannot find any notices of William's death or any divorce. Perhaps she was a bigamist?

Sarah married Thomas Waters(1849-1917) in 1903. Thomas was 54 years old at the time and Sarah was 36. According to the electoral rolls, Thomas worked as a labourer and they lived at 2 Church Street, Port Melbourne.

Thomas died in 1917.

Sarah was living at 2 Church Street, Port Melbourne in 1915 and in 1927 was found living at 201 Heath Street, Port Melbourne. (according to the electoral rolls)

201 Heath Street,

Port Melbourne.

Sarah died 21st November, 1935 in the Alfred Hospital, and was buried in the Coburg, Victoria cemetery.

I have included a copy of her death certificate on the following page. Its interesting that on the certificate, Sarah Ann and Violet Lily Myrtle's births are credited to Thomas Waters rather than William Garlepp. Both their birth certificates have William listed as the father. Perhaps, William didn't actually return after he was charged with desertion and Sarah had the children with Thomas but because she was still married, registered them with William as the father?

THIRD SCHEDULE.

10377

DEATHS in the District of MELBOURNE, in Victoria, Registered by SAMUEL HENRY EDGERTON HOLLOW.

1 No.	10377
Description—	
2 When and where died	21st November, 1935, Alfred Hospital, Prahran, City of Melbourne, County of Bourke. U.R. 121 Station Street, Port Melbourne, City of Port Melbourne.
3 Name and surname ... ... Occupation	Sarah Ann WATERS, Not Any.
4 Sex and age	Female, 68 years.
5 (1) Cause of death ... ... (2) Duration of last illness ... (3) Legally qualified medical practitioner by whom certified ... and (4) When he last saw deceased ...	Chronic myocarditis — weeks, Broncho-pneumonia, Medullary failure — hours, Dr. N.Laidlaw, 21st November, 1935.
6 Name and surname of father and mother (maiden name, if known), with occupation	John French, Ellen French, formerly O'Halleron, Shipping Providore.
7 Signature, description, and residence of informant	[signature] Authorized Agent, Alfred Hospital, Prahran.
8 (1) Signature of Registrar ... (2) Date ... ... and (3) Where registered	[signature] 26th November, 1935. Melbourne.
If burial registered—	
9 When and where buried ... Undertaker by whom certified ...	23rd November, 1935, Coburg Cemetery, A.W.Aldridge, acting for Hayboulds Proprietary Limited.
10 Name and religion of Minister, or names of witnesses of burial ...	E.Henton, B.F.Sulliven.
11 Where born, and how long in the Australian States, stating which	New South Wales, 67 years in Victoria, Unknown period in New South Wales.
If deceased was married— 12 (1) Where ... . and (2) At what age ... ... and (3) To whom ... ... 13 Issue in order of birth, the names and ages	First Marriage :— Benalla, Victoria, 18 years, William Garlepp, deceased.. Issue :— Mary Agnes, 49 years, William George, 47 years, Ernest Edward, 45 years, (One Child, deceased, Name, and Sex, (Unknown.
	Second Marriage :— Melbourne, Victoria, Unknown, Thomas Waters, deceased. Issue :— Sarah Ann, 41 years, Violet Lily Myrtle, 36 years.

10377

In 1906, Mary Agnes, Sarah's first daughter, married John Buckley (1876-1959) They had the following children:

Thomas James Buckley   1909–1959
John Edward Buckley Jr   1911–1980
Earnest William Kenneth Buckley   1911–1979

In 1920 Mary Agnes had another child however the fathers name wasn't on the birth certificate and she had used her maiden name of Garlepp.

John Patrick Garlepp   1920-1984

In 1949 John married Florence Mary Bisset   1926–1980

On Patrick's death certificate it has Mary Ring as his mother.

In 1908 William George, William and Sarah's eldest son, married Alma Veronika Noonan or Neenan (1890-1949) at Sts Peter and Paul Catholic church, in South Melbourne.   I have included a copy of their marriage certificate on   the next page and a picture of the church below.

William and Alma had the following children:

William Austin Garlepp   1908–1982
Ernest John Garlepp   1909–1993
Alice Veronika Garlepp   1912–1998
Nellie Murial Olive Garlepp   1913–1988
Thomas George Garlepp   1917–1999
Freda Violet Myrtle Garlepp   1918–1998
Kathleen Alma Garlepp   1922-2013
Lillian May Garlepp   1924–1995
John Joseph Garlepp   1927–1957

In the State of Victoria

In the Commonwealth of Australia.

FOURTH SCHEDULE. STS Nos. 2691 and 2720.—FORM A.

CERTIFICATE OF MARRIAGE. [A.

Year 1908   Parish or Church District   South Melbourne   Catholic

(1)	(2)	(3)	(4)		
679	31st July 1908 S. Peter & Paul's South Melb.	William Garlepp	Bachelor	–	Port Melb.
		Alma Veronica Neenan	Spinster	–	Launceston

Occupation. (8)	Age in years (last Birthday) (9)	Present. (10)	Usual. (11)	Father. Also Occupation. (12)	Mother. (Full Maiden Name.) (13)
Hake Maker	20	101 Dow St. Port Melbourne		Wm Garlepp Labourer	Sara French
Domestic	18	17 Thistlewaite St. Sth Melb.		Wm Neenan Labourer	Alice Smith

<table>
<tr><td rowspan="6">Father.
(1) Name of Celebrant,
(2) Designation and Denomination (e.g., a minister of the Roman Catholic Church),
(3) Strike out these words if inapplicable,
(4) Name and relationship to minor (e.g., "John Jones, father of the bride")</td>
<td>We declare that the above is a true statement of the particulars relating to each of us respectively; and that Marriage (1) by license was solemnized between us on the date and at the place mentioned, according to (2) the rite of the Catholic Church</td>
<td>William Garlepp

Alma Veronica Neenan

Signatures of Parties.</td></tr>
</table>

Signatures of Witnesses — Ernest Garlepp / Corral Waldron

I, (3) T. F. O'Sullevan _____ being (4) a Catholic Priest do hereby certify that I have this day duly celebrated Marriage between the abovenamed parties, after notice (5) had been dispensed with by permission of _____ Esq., J.P.), and after declaration, duly made as by law required [5]and with the written consent of (6) Sara Waters, mother of Wm Garlepp & Wm Neenan father of the bride

Dated this Thirty-First day of July 190

Signature of Minister, Government Statist, or Registrar of Marriages.   T. F. O'Sullevan

N.241/1115.—14613.

I found this little article in the Standard on 21 August, 1909 about Alma.
I'm pretty sure that May Prideaux was
a relative of the Garlepps.

William George enlisted in the Army during the second world war on 22 January, 1940.

He gave his birthday as 3 October, 1890. His birth certificate is registered in 1887. Either he didn't know for sure when his birth year was, or else he wanted to seem 3 years younger. He was 52 at the time.

I have attached all his war records on the next few pages. Below are pictures of the medals he received.

War Medal

Australian Service Medal

A.A. Form Mob. 1

AUSTRALIAN ⁂ MILITARY FORCES

M. F.

MOBILIZATION ATTESTATION FORM

To be filled in for all Persons at the Place of Assembly when called out under Parts III. or IV. of the Defence Act, or when voluntarily enlisted.

Army No. *V82·733*

Surname *GARLEPP* (BLOCK CAPITALS) Christian Names *William George*

Unit *Garrison Depot.*

Command Recruiting Depot

Enlisted for war service at Sturt St., South Melbourne, S.C.4 (Place)

Victoria (State) *22ⁿᵈ January 40.* (Date)

A

Questions to be put to persons called out or presenting themselves for voluntary enlistment.*

1. What is your name? ... ...
{ 1. Surname *GARLEPP* (BLOCK LETTERS)
  Other names *William George*

2. Where were you born? ... ...
{ 2. In or near the town of *Port Melbne*
  in the state or country of *Victoria*

3. Are you a British Subject? ... ...
3. *Yes*

4. What is your age and date of birth? ... ...
{ 4. Age *49½ Years*
  Date of Birth *3/10/1890*

5. What is your trade or occupation? ... ...
5. *Stevedore*

6. Are you married, single or widower? ...
6. *Married*

7. Have you previously served on active service? If so, where and in what arm? ... ...
} 7. *29ᵗʰ Batt A.I.F. Nᵒ 5123*

8. Who is your actual next of kin? (Order of relationship:—wife, eldest son, eldest daughter, father, mother, eldest brother, eldest sister, eldest half-brother, eldest half-sister) ...
{ 8. Name *Alma Veronica Garlepp*
  Address *33 St Vincents St*
  Albert Park
  Relationship *Wife*

9. What is your permanent address? ... ...
{ 9. *33 St Vincents St*
  Albert Park

10. What is your religious denomination? (This question need not be answered if the man has a conscientious objection to doing so) ... ...
} 10. *R. C.*

I, *William George Garlepp* do solemnly declare that the above answers made by me to the above questions are true.

Witnessed by *C McPherson Lieut*
(Signature of Attesting or Witnessing Officer)

W. G. Garlepp
Signature

JAN 22 1940

The person will be warned that should he give false answers to any of these questions he will be liable to heavy penalties under the Defence Act.

D.34?/?/?.—C.4778.—100M

B

MEDICAL EXAMINATION

nade full and careful examination of the abovenamed person in accordance with the instructions contained in the

s for Australian Army Medical Services. In my opinion he is—*

I.

~~unfit for Class I †~~ ....

II.   *Nil class 2   B.P. extroved*
                                                       teeth satisfactory

~~unfit for Class II †~~ ....

litary service † .... *B. P. teeth*

AREA, 5.   Date *22-1-40*

      Signature of Examining Medical Officer   *St Allen*

      * Classifications which are inapplicable to be struck out.   † Reasons for unfitness to be stated.

C

OATH OF ENLISTMENT ‡

sons voluntarily enlisted or called upon under Part III. or Part IV. of the Defence Act to serve in the Citizen

e of war. Not compulsory for serving members of the Forces or those allotted to the Citizen Forces

II. of the Act, but unless in any case an objection is raised, the oath should be administered to them as

remony of attestation.

illiam George Garlepp _____ swear that I will well and truly

overeign Lord, the King, in the Military Forces of the Commonwealth of Australia until the

the present time of war or until sooner lawfully discharged, dismissed, or removed, and that I

is Majesty's enemies and cause His Majesty's peace to be kept and maintained, and that I will

s appertaining to my service faithfully discharge my duty according to law.

𝖘𝖔 𝕳𝖊𝖑𝖕 𝕸𝖊 𝕲𝖔𝖉 !

Signature of Person Enlisted   *W. G. Garlepp*

ibed at Sturt St., South Melbourne, S.C. in the State of _____ *Victoria*

enty fifth _____ day of _____ *January* _____ 19 *40*

me—

Signature of Attesting Officer   *W J McPherson Lieut.*

s who object to take an oath may make an affirmation in accordance with the Third Schedule of the Defence Act.   In

bove form will be amended accordingly and initialed by the Attesting Officer.

T. Rider. Acting Govt. Printer, Melb.

73.—100M.

AF. B.103—1 (Adapted)

SERVICE AND CASUALTY FORM

Army No. V82,733

Unit 2 Garrn. Depot.

Surname **GARLEPP** (Block Capitals)

Rank **Pte.** Christian Names **William George** Ord.No.
(On Enlistment)

Date of Enlistment 22/1/40 Mob. Pt.2.

Place **Melbourne**

Date of Birth **3/10/1890**

Place of Birth **Port Melbourne**

Trade or Occupation **Stevedore**

Religion **R.C.**

Marital Condition **Married**

Next of Kin **Alma Veronica Garlepp**

Address of Next of Kin **33 St. Vincents St.**
Albert Park.

Relationship **Wife**

Identification—Colour of Hair **Fair** Eyes **Hazel**
Distinctive Marks **Tattoo marks L. fore-arm.**
Scar rt. knee. " shin.

Medical Classification— Class I. Class II.
(On Enlistment)

REPORT		Record of all casualties regarding promotions (acting, temporary, local or substantive), appointments, transfers, postings, attachments, &c., forfeiture of pay, wounds, accidents, admission to and discharge from Hospital, Casualty Clearing Stations, &c. Date of disembarkation and embarkation from a theatre of war (including furlough, &c.).	Date of Casualty	Place of Casualty	Authority W3011, B.2003, or other Document	Signature of Officer Certifying Correctness of Entries
Date	From whom received					
25-1-40	12th Gar Bn	Taken on Strength D.O. 9/3/40	25-1-40	Bn Meadows	W30" 22/2/40	
24-3-41	"	Granted a Ac. Tegni. Trans. 24-8-44 To	8-4-41	"	Rort 3	
16-11-41	"	(unt4 6 days) A.R.R.S. Adm. from 14-11-41 K	20-11-41	"	Ro.112/4A/5	
29-11-41	"	Adl. to 6/Hosp B.medero (Bron. Pneumonia)	27-11-41	"	Ro.116-41-5	
"	"	Transft. to 115 Gen Hos from 6/Hosp.	27-11-41	"	Ro.119/41/10	
12-12-41	"	" 107 Gen Det from NS.G.H.	10-12-41	"		
19-12-41	"	Marched in from 107 Gen Depot	13-12-41	"	Ro.120-41-5	
15-12-41	R.J Camp	Marched out to 12 Years Pstn	15-12-41	Caulfield		
15-12-41	" "	Resumes duit from R.J. Camp.	15-12-41	"	Ro.120-41-5	
22-2-43	12 Gar Bn	Medical Category from B2 to B N	16-2-43	Broadff	Ro.7/43/5	
		Vic: Lateral per brown with subfrequelae				
11-3-43	S.D.D.	Ceases and. 6 I.D.U.		Tocks	Ro.27/43/5 11-3-43	
15-3-43	S.D.D.	attr from 13 Gan Bn		Enfield	Ro.15/43/51 11-3-43	

NOTHING TO BE WRITTEN IN THIS SPACE.

79

V82733 573
Garlyle

NOTHING TO BE WRITTEN IN THIS SPACE.

REPORT		Record of all casualties regarding promotions (acting, temporary, local or substantive), appointments, transfers, postings, attachments, &c., forfeiture of pay, wounds, accidents, admission to, and discharge from Hospital, Casualty Clearing Stations, &c., Date of disembarkation and embarkation from a theatre of war (including furlough, &c.).	Date of Casualty	Place of Casualty	Authority W.3011, B.2069, or other Document	Signature of Officer Certifying Correctness of Entries
Date	From whom received					
14-3-43	S.D.R.	Discharged Auth...	24/3/43	field	N3011 657/43	M Crock

GRATUITY CHECKED 21 FEB 1949

12.3434/5.39.—C.4796.

VICTORIA L OF C AREA.   FORM A.1.

PROCEEDINGS of DISCHARGE.
(To be compiled by Reception Camp and forwarded to Records Office
on completion of Discharge.)

Vic L of C Area Authy. 764 Date 24 2 43 A.M.R. & O. V1.

NAME (in full) GARLEPP. William George.
(SURNAME block.)
NO. V 82733 RANK Pte UNIT 12 Aust Gen Bn.

CERT OF DISCHARGE NO. 22271   WIDOWER, Married, Single (Cross out
                                                           as required,)

Discharge at Reception Camp, Caulfield on_____

o/c to Post - 7/17   As at   20 . 3 . 43 .
        No one to sign it   (7 Days).

2 MEDICAL PARTICULARS of DISCHARGE (To be compiled by examing M.O.)

   AGE 57   HEIGHT 5' 11½" COMPLEXION   Medium

   EYES Blue HAIR Grey - DISTINCTIVE_____
                              MARKS
   I certify that the soldier named above, on the date of Discharge
   DID/DID NOT claim or reveal a disability caused or aggravated by WAR
   SERVICE. (Strike out DID or DID NOT AS APPLICABLE.)
   Where such a disability was claimed or revealed, the matter has been
   investigated by a Medical Board.
   Signature of EXAMING OFFICER,_____

   In cases where the disability has not been investigated Discharged
   will be deferred.

3
   REASON FOR DISCHARGED___V1_____

   Total period of Service towards Completion of Engagements 1151 Days,
              Including Service Abroad of   540   Days.

   Total Place of residence after Discharge to which D/C may be posted is
        33 St Vincent St Albert Park.

4. UNIFORM RETURNED NO PLAIN CLOTHES ISSUED NO   OR

   DESPATCHED TO_____ BY K Hull ON 13 · 3 · 43

5 CERTIFICATE TO BE SIGNED BY SOLDIER ON DISCHARGED.

   I hereby acknowledge that I have received all my Pay, Allowances, and
   Clothing, all just demands, up to the present date, subject to the
   reservations of the claims noted on the reserve side therewith,

   PLACE_____CAULFIELD   H.G. Garlepp
                                        (Signature of Soldier)
   DATE   13. 3 43
                                        (Signature of Witness)

6 CONFIRMATION OF DISCHARGE.
   I have impartially inquired into all matters brought before me in
   accordance with regulations and hereby confirm the Discharge.

   PLACE   CAULFIELD
         13. 3. 43.   (Signature & appointment of
                                              confirming Officer.)
   Discharge in absentia.   Certificate of Discharge placed in

   Cert. of Discharge posted to_____ on_____ Personal File.

   Date of Embarkation.   Date of Disembarkation.

   Bilateral ?as ?avous ? ?ature ?ig??us PTE 810 NU

NAA: B884, V82733

NAME GARLEPP W. G. No. V 83733

Address

1	1939/45 STAR			
2	AFRICA STAR		Recorder	
3	„ with 1st Clasp		Checker	
4	„ with 8th Clasp		AWARDS WITHHELD	
5	ATLANTIC STAR		Serials:	
6	A.C. EUROPE STAR		REASON:	
7	ITALY STAR			
8	FRANCE & G. STAR			
9	PACIFIC STAR		AUTHORITY:	
10	BURMA STAR			
11	DEFENCE MEDAL			
12	WAR MEDAL	✓		
13	A.S.M.	✓	Packer	
14	ASB		Despatcher	

TO WHOM DESPATCHED

Reg'd Parcel No. .... DATE...........................

RECEIPT

Serials...................... Sig............................

AHQ Press—3443—9/46—710m .... DATE........................

National Archives of Australia   NAA: B884, V82733

Alma Veronica died in 1949.   The notices were placed in the Age newspaper on 8 March 1949.
She was 59 years old.

GARLEPP. — On March 7, at her
home, 33 St. Vincent-street, Albert
Park, Alma Veronica, the dearly be-
loved wife of William Garlepp, and de-
voted mother of William, Ernest, Alice,
Nellie, Freda, Kathleen, Lillian, Jack,
Thomas and Robert, aged 59 years.
Requiescat in pace.

GARLEPP. — On March 7, beloved
mother of Billy, and mother-in-law
of Gladys, loving nannie of Janice and
Sharyn. Always remembered.

GARLEPP.—Alma, dearly loved sister-
in-law of Tom, auntie of Tommy
Nell and Allie Waldron. Sadly missed.
—Waldron, Ringwood East.

William continued to live at 33 St Vincent Street, Albert Park working as a Stevedore and finally as
a foreman. He died 5 July, 1964 and was buried at the Fawkner cemetery.

On 16 December, 1933, Ernest John, the second eldest child of William and Alma was in the newspaper and being called a hero.

The following article was found in the News (Adelaide, SA : 1923 - 1954), on Saturday 16 December 1933

WORKLESS MAN HERO OF FIRE

Vanished for Week After Saving Baby

MELBOURNE, Saturday.—An unemployed motor driver, Mr E J. Garlepp, aged 23, of Albert Park, was found last night to have been the hero of last Saturday night's South Melbourne fire, in which a baby was saved from being burnt to death in dramatic circumstances.

Mr. Garlepp was on his way home from a picture show when he noticed a strong light on the balcony of a house in Cardigan place, South Melbourne Hearing screams, he broke down the door, rushed up two flights of stairs, and saved a baby from a burning settee He aroused Mr. H Hardy, the father of the child, and between them they extinguished the flames Then Mr Garlepp disappeared unknown

Mr Garlepp called at Mr Hardy's home last night, and asked after the baby's health. It was the first opportunity the grateful parents had had of offering their thanks, and discovering the identity of the rescuer

"I went home after rescuing the baby because I did not want to boast about it or appear in the limelight," said Mr Garlepp

A week later on 23 December, 1933 the article was printed in the Emerald Record. I have transcribed it on the following page for easier reading

Rescuer Reveals His Identity

CHIEF ACTOR IN SAVE FROM BURNING HOUSE

Mr. E. J. Garlepp, an unemployed motor driver, who lives in St. Vincent street, was recently returning home from a picture show with a lady friend, when, passing a house in Cardigan Place, he noticed a strong light in a window, and heard screams. He broke down the door, and hurried upstairs, where he rescued a baby from a burning settee. He then roused the father of the child, Mr. H. Hardy, and between them they extinguished the flames. Mr. Garlepp then left without disclosing his identity, which was not discovered until some days later, when he called on Mr. Hardy to discover how the child was getting on The parents were glad to express their gratitude to Mr. Garlepp for his splendid services.

Speaking of the event, Mr. Garlepp said there were many people present at the time, but no one seemed inclined to do anything to rescue the baby, or extinguish the flames.

The baby is still in the Children's Hospital.

Mr. Hardy said he had not the means to compensate Mr. Garlepp, otherwise he would do so.

Rescuer Reveals His Identity

CHIEF ACTOR IN SAVE FROM BURNING HOUSE

Mr. E. J. Garlepp, an unemployed motor driver, who lives in St. Vincent street, was recently returning home from a picture show with a lady friend, when, passing a house in Cardigan Place, he noticed a strong light in a window, and heard screams. He broke down the door, and hurried upstairs, where he rescued a baby from a burning settee. He then roused the father of the child, Mr. H. Hardy, and between them they extinguished the flames.

Mr. Garlepp then left without disclosing his identity, which was not discovered until some days , later, when he called on Mr. Hardy to discover how the child was getting on. The parents were glad to express their gratitude to Mr. Garlepp for his splendid services. Speaking of the event, Mr. Garlepp said there were many people present at the time, but no one seemed inclined to do anything to rescue the baby, or extinguish the flames. The baby is still in the Children's Hospital. , Mr. Hardy said he had not the means to compensate Mr. Garlepp, otherwise he would do so.

BABY SAVED FROM FLAMES

Balcony Fire Rescue

Telling how he awoke to find flames *[text faded and partially illegible]* ... Mr. Henry Hardy, an engineer, of Cardigan Street, Albert Park, said today that in another few minutes his child would have been burned to death.

He bounded out of bed to save the baby, but a man who had dashed through a kitchenette snatched the child from the burning settee. This man had rushed from a group of 50 or 60 people who gathered in front of the house, raced up two flights of stairs, saved the baby, and handed her to Mrs Heffner, a neighbour, for first-aid treatment. He vanished inside three minutes without telling anyone who he was.

The infant, Joyce Hardy, 14 months old, is in the Children's Hospital suffering from burns on the leg and foot. Her father had his hands and arms burned in trying to beat out the flames from the burning bedclothes.

SMOKING A CIGARETTE

"I'm feeling very worried and shaken today," said Mr Hardy. "Little Joyce is our only child. We turn a settee with a back to it to the wall and make a sort of cot out of it for her. The baby and I slept on the balcony because my wife had a girl visitor. My wife and the girl went to the pictures on Saturday night.

"I had been working pretty hard and was very tired. At 9 o'clock I put the baby to bed on the balcony. I was smoking a cigarette and, to be perfectly candid, I think some cigarette ash must have fallen on the clothes of little Joyce's bed. I stayed up for a short while listening to the wireless.

"When I went to bed there was no sign of fire on the balcony. I don't know exactly when it started. The kapok must have smouldered for a good while. The baby in her settee was sleeping near my bed. Usually if she makes the slightest sound I wake. But on Saturday night I was extra tired."

BEDCLOTHES BLAZING

"Shouting from the street and the noise of someone running through the flat awakened me at 10.25 p.m. I awoke bewildered. Flames were rising higher than the balcony railing. The fire seemed all round me. My first thought was for the baby. I flung off bedclothes that were blazing, but at that moment a man who seemed to be between 30 and 40 years old, plucked the child out of the burning settee. The blanket was on fire under her and the quilt, pillows and cushions were blazing. The little nightdress was on fire at the edges.

"I'm sorry I did not get the man's name. He was game all right, because in a strange house he did not know but that he would meet more fire inside. Yet he disappeared as quickly as he arrived.

"Mrs Heffner put oil on the baby's little foot and leg, and I had a lively five minutes trying to put out the blazing bedclothes.

"We were decidedly lucky. Five minutes later and it would have been much worse."

"You can imagine my feelings" said Mrs Hardy, "when I was on my way home and the firemen passed me. Someone said to me 'A baby has been burned to death on a balcony.' I knew little Joyce would be sleeping on the balcony and I nearly collapsed when I saw the crowd outside the house where we have a flat.

"I struggled through a press of people outside and then someone said, 'A baby has fallen from the balcony.' It was a terrible experience."

The article to the left appeared in the Herald on Monday 11 December 1933

I have transcribed it on the following page for easier reading.

The one below was in the Daily Mercury, QLD 12 December, 1933

RESCUE OF CHILD.

BY UNKNOWN MAN.

WHO IMMEDIATELY DISAPPEARED.

MELBOURNE, Dec. 11.—Somewhere in Melbourne there is a modest hero, who though unknown, was the means of saving a baby's life when a house caught fire in Albert Park yesterday.

The occupant of the house, Henry Hardy, was asleep when he was awakened by the screams of his 14 months-old daughter who had been asleep on a settee on the balcony outside. He groped his way through the smoke-filled room, where an unknown man was tearing the burning clothes from the child.

"Not a moment too soon," said the man, and handing the baby to the care of a woman, who followed him, disappeared.

The man had rushed from a group of people who had gathered in front of the house when the outbreak occurred.

Mr. Hardy said to-day that if the rescuer had been five seconds later, neither the baby nor he would have escaped alive.

The child was taken to the hospital with severe body burns.

BABY SAVED from flames

Balcony Fire Rescue

Telling how he awoke to find flames racing across the quilt of his own bed and leaping up from the settee where his baby daughter slept on the balcony.

Mr Henry Hardy, an engineer, of Cardigan Street, Albert Park, said today that in another few minutes his child would have been burned to death. He bounded out of bed to save the baby, but a man who had dashed through a kitchenette snatched the child from the burning settee. This man had rushed from a group of 50 or 60 people who gathered in front of the house, raced up two flights of stairs, saved the baby, and handed her to Mrs Heffner, a neighbor, for first-aid treatment. He vanished inside three minutes without telling anyone who he was. The infant, Joyce Hardy, 14 months old, is in the Children's Hospital suffering from burns on the leg and foot. Her father had his hands and arm burned in trying to beat out the flames from the burning bedclothes.

SMOKING A CIGARETTE

"I'm feeling very worried and shaken today," said Mr Hardy. "Little Joyce is our only child. We turn a settee with a back to It to the wall and make a sort of cot out of it for her. The baby and I slept on the balcony because my wife had a girl visitor. My wife and the girl went to the pictures on Saturday night. "I had been working pretty hard and was very tired. At 9 o clock I put the baby to bed on the balcony. I was smoking a cigarette and, to be perfectly candid, I think some cigarette ash must have fallen on the clothes of little Joyce's bed. I stayed up for a short while listening to the wireless. "When I went to bed there was no sign of fire on the balcony. I don't know exactly when it started. The kapok must have smouldered for a good while. The baby in her settee was sleeping near my bed. Usually if she makes the slightest sound I wake. But on Saturday night I was extra tired.

" BEDCLOTHES BLAZING

"Shouting from the street and the noise of someone running through the fiat awakened me at 10.25 p.m. I awoke bewildered. Flames were rising higher than the balcony railing. The fire seemed all round me. My first thought was for the baby. I flung off bedclothes that were blazing, but at that moment a man, who seemed to be between 30 and 40 years old, plucked the child out of the burning settee. The blanket was on fire under her and the quilt, pillows and cushions were blazing. The little nightdress was on fire at the edges. "I'm sorry I did not get the man's name. He was game all right, because in a strange house he did not know but that he would meet more fire inside. Yet he disappeared as quickly as he arrived. "Mrs Heffner put oil on the baby's little foot and leg, and I had a lively five minutes trying to put out the blazing bedclothes. "We "We were decidedly lucky. Five minutes later and it would have been much worse." "You can imagine my feelings," said Mrs Hardy, "when I was on my way home and the firemen passed me. Someone said to me 'A baby has been burned to death on a balcony. I knew little Joyce would be sleeping on the balcony and I nearly collapsed when I saw the crowd outside the house where we have a flat. "I struggled through a press of people outside and then someone said, 'A baby has fallen from the balcony. It was a terrible experience."

In March, 1957, John Joseph, the 8th child of William and Alma was accidentally shot dead by his companion. The below small article was the only information that I could find on this incident.

William Austin Garlepp (1908-1992), William and Alma's eldest child played for Port Melbourne.

I contacted the club and was told that he played 25 senior games for the club starting in 1833.

The photo below is the team. I'm not sure which one is William.

On the following page is the team sheet.

Unfortunately he wasn't part of a premiership during the years he played.

I love this little article found in The Herald, 16 January, 1933.

Man Shot Dead On Quail Shoot

MELBOURNE, Sunday —A 35-year-old Melbourne man was accidentally shot dead by one of his companions while quail shooting at Lara, near Geelong, yesterday.

He was John Garlepp, of St. Vincent's Place, Albert Park, who was shot through the head with a 12 gauge shotgun.

W. GARLEPP is consistently good on the wing for Port Melbourne. He is fast to the ball and has a big advantage in being very sure in the air. He asserted this aerial superiority on Saturday when he was opposed by Rogers (Coburg). The pair broke about even on the day, the Ports player being seen at his best in the aerial duels. Rogers was one of a strong centre line for Coburg. Hogan and Willox were not beaten.

Garlepp

ASSOCIATION FOOTBALL RECORDER.

TO-DAY'S TEAMS

Umpires.—Boundary: W. Clifton, J. Martin.
Goal: F. Durant, W. Macpherson.

PORT MELBOURNE.

	Name.	Age.	Hgt. ft. in.	Wgt. st. lbs.
1	W. Lovett (c.)	29	5.8	10.0
2	S. Plumridge	26	5.7	11.3
3	E. Perritt	26	6.0½	14.2
4	W. Bedford	25	5.9½	12.0
5	H. Lowrie	21	5.10	12.12
6	E. Leggo	22	6.0	12.3
7	T. Murphy	24	5.11	11.12
9	J. Garbutt	29	6.1	12.6
10	A. Maltby	19	5.9	11.12
11	L. Boquest	20	5.10	11.8
12	R. Julier	22	5.8	11.2
13	A. Bills	22	6.2	13.4
14	T. Brooker	24	5.7	11.0
15	P. Bolman	21	5.3	10.0
16	J. Rusden	19	5.11	9.9
17	K. Aldridge	23	6.0	12.12
18	J. Tuite	23	5.10½	13.10
20	J. Landorf	21	5.11½	13.0
21	C. Keating	24	5.8½	11.0
22	W. Payne	21	5.11½	10.12
23	P. May	25	5.7	11.7
24	L. Keating	21	5.6½	10.2
26	W. Garlepp	23	5.7	10.0
27	T. Lahiff	22	5.5	10.9
28	— Atkinson	26	5.11	11.8
29	W. Rees	32	6.3	15.3

NORTHCOTE.

	Name.	Age.	Hgt. ft. in.	Wgt. st. lbs.
1	P. Rowe (c.)	36	6.1	13.10
2	A. Gray	24	5.7	9.9
3	R. Ross	24	5.2	9.6
4	P. Brown	26	5.8	11.8
5	R. Humphries	22	5.11	12.7
6	E. Hart	21	5.11	11.5
7	L. Smith	21	5.10	11.10
8	F. Ackland	22	5.10	12.12
11	J. Flinn	24	6.0½	13.10
12	T. Corrigan	29	5.10	12.0
13	A. Connell	20	6.0	12.9
14	S. Wilson	20	5.11	11.2
15	E. Bray	23	5.4	11.0
16	G. Simmonds	23	5.8½	10.7
17	R. Byrne	26	5.10	13.7
19	C. Williamson	19	6.1	13.8
20	F. Seymour	28	5.11	11.5
21	S. Powell	23	5.9½	10.8
23	J. Woods	27	5.10	12.9
24	T. Garrett	25	5.7	10.7
25	R. Goullet	28	6.0	13.7

DANCERS! Football is nearly over; but, remember, you can enjoy
OLD-STYLE DANCING
EVERY EVENING AT THE PALAIS ROYAL.
See "Age" Daily.

Violet Lillian Myrtle Garlepp was born 14 February 1898. Her birth certificate states that William and Sarah Garlepp are her parents. It would appear that William wasn't around long after she was born. There is no death registered for him. Her mother Sarah married Thomas Waters when Violet was around 5 years old and she seems to have taken on the Waters name as her own, as when she married William James Eldridge in 1917 she states that is her surname. They were married at the Broadmeadows Army Camp.

In 1918 a daughter is born to Violet, Iris Myra Kathleen Eldridge. On Iris' birth registration, it states that father is unknown. Iris died in 1978, apparently unmarried and again her father is unknown.

In 1921 another child is born to Violet. Agnes Myrle Eldridge lived for just one day. Again the mother is Violet Waters and the father is unknown.

James was about 40 years of age when he married the 19 year old Violet.

James William Eldridge was born at Camberwell, Surrey, England the son of James William Eldridge and Mary Hall. James and his sister Eliza Annie were living with their parents at 19 Davey Street, Camberwell when the 1881 British census was taken. His father was a dairyman born at Camberwell.

James must have migrated to Australia as on 1 Jul 1915 he enlisted in the Australian Military Forces at Melbourne, Victoria. He was a stoker and he showed his age as 37 and his birthplace as Peckham, London England. He was discharged in Oct 1915 as medically unfit due to a loose body in his right knee joint aggravated by marching. On 20 August 1917 he again enlisted at Melbourne, Victoria. He was then shown as a stevedore aged 39 1/2.

On 19 Nov 1917 he married to Violet Lily Myrtle Waters at the Broadmeadows Camp . He was shown as being aged 38 and his father as deceased and Violet as being aged 19.

James William was a Private, Service Number 7635, in the 8th Battalion, AIF. He embarked from Melbourne per A71 "Nestor" on 21 Nov 1917 for England and he marched to the AIF Training Battalion at Sutton Veny on 9 Jan 1918 following his arrival. On 27 Mar 1918 he went absent without leave. On 7 May 1918 a Court of Inquiry was held and he was later formally discharged from the AIF on 1 April 1920. No record of his death is known.

In the 1919 electoral roll, James is living Off Dow Street, Port Melbourne and Violet is living 39 Esplanade, Port Melbourne. In the 1922 electoral roll, they are again living apart. I find it interesting that we have no more information about James past this point. He may have gone back to England.

Violet then remarried on 25 Nov 1922 to David Alexander Walker (1887-1935) , son of Alexander Walker(1857 -1942) and Mary Ann (nee Power 1862-1922). When Violet remarried she was shown as a widow as of 20 May 1918!

David was born in 1887 at Port Melbourne, the first of three children of Alexander Walker and Mary Ann Walker nee Power. He lived in Port Melbourne and worked as a stevedore and was a talented amateur boxer. During World War 1 he joined the AIF following a campaign of recruitment aimed at sportsmen called the "sportsmen's 1000). He enlisted in 1917 and was sent to training camp at Broadmeadows.

David was posted overseas and in 1918 embarked on the "Euripides" on the 1st of May and headed for England. During the voyage he won a boxing tournament and was awarded a gold fob watch as a prize.

He never saw any action in the war but was posted to France for a short time after the war. Back in England he was sent to Sutton Veny where in 1919 he won the Regiment's boxing Championship during the Anzac sports. He was presented with the trophy as Champion by Albert Jacka VC.

David returned to Australia on board the "Chemitz" later in 1919.

Here are a couple of pics of David.

AUSTRALIAN WAR MEMORIAL   P00563.001

He married Violet Lily Myrtle on the 25 of November 1922 at Port Melbourne. They lived in Port Melbourne where David again worked as a stevedore and they had six children:

Leslie	1923-
Cyril	1924-1924
Daniel	1927-1927
John	1929-
Donald	1930-2020
Lillian	1934-

WITHOUT THE OPTION.

Wife-Beater Sent to Gaol.

David Alexander Walker, 38 years, stevedore's laborer, was charged at South Melbourne yesterday with having assaulted his wife.

Mrs. Walker said she did not wish to proceed with the case.

Mr. Smith, P.M.: Did he assault you?

Complainant: Yes. He knocked me down, and struck me in the face several times.

Mr. Smith said the bench would hear the evidence.

Walker said he was nursing the baby on Saturday evening, when complainant made a very offensive remark to him. He jumped on to his feet, and, running against her, they both fell down.

Mr. Smith, in sentencing accused to seven days' imprisonment, said Walker would not be given the option of paying a fine. It seemed to be useless to impose fines on men convicted of assaulting their wives.

Walker said he would appeal.

On 3 June, 1926, the Age reported that David was sentenced 7 days in gaol for assaulting Violet. Pictured to the left.

On 23 May 1933 David was again convicted of assault on Violet and was sentenced to one month imprisonment. The Age reported this, see below.

Woman Who Resented an Indelicate Remark.

David Alexander Walker, 45 years, laborer, Gladstone-street, Montague, was charged at Port Melbourne court yesterday with having assaulted his wife.

Evidence was given that Mrs. Walker resented an indelicate remark her husband made in the presence of a lodger, and that when both men laughed at her discomfiture she threw a cup of tea over defendant. The latter then brutally attacked her.

Accused denied that he had struck his wife, asserting that she had fallen against the furniture.

Walker admitted a previous conviction for assaulting his wife. He was sentenced to one month's imprisonment.

During the depression in the 1930's David was out of work and went looking for a job in the country. While he was away, Violet left home with the children and disappeared. David returned to the city and went looking for them but apparently being unsuccessful became depressed and committed suicide after drinking Lysol at his Mother in Law's house. He died in Prince Henry Hospital on 3 September 1935, aged 48 and was buried in the Brighton Cemetery.

I have included the depositions of Sarah, Violet's mother, and Lavinia, Ernest's wife on the next few pages with transcriptions.

DEPOSITION OF A WITNESS

DEPOSITION OF A WITNESS

Sarah Waters

Sarah Waters

Deposition of a Witness.

The Deponent: Sarah Ann Waters

On her oath saith, I am a Widow residing at 121 Station Street, Port Melbourne.

I had known the deceased David Alexander Walker of 14 Spring Street, Port Melbourne for the past 40 years. He was my son in law.

He was a married man and in receipt of sustenance. On the morning of the 3rd day of September 1935,

sometime after 10.30 o'clock the deceased came to my home under the influence of intoxicating liquor. He sat on the side of my bed and I sat alongside of him. He had a bottle of wine which he took from under his coat, and said, Here Mum, I have brought you a bottle of wine. I took the bottle of wine and placed it on the chest of drawers. I don't know how much wine was in the bottle, neither did I drink any of it. Deceased then took a small bottle similar to the one, produced, and poured some of the contents into a cup I had got for him. I did not know what the small bottle contained. He then swallowed the contents of the cup and said, that's done it. He then fell backwards across the bed with his feet resting on the floor. I then looked at the bottle and saw the word lysol on it. I suspected he had taken poison, and I got salt and water in a cup and gave it to him and he drank it, then vomited on the floor. I then got the floor cloth and wiped up the vomit. I then took the cup and which he had drunk the lysol out of and smashed it into pieces in the dust tin in the yard, for the fear the children may get hold of it. A few minutes later my daughter in law, Mrs Garlepp who resides with me came home and I told her that I believed my son in law had taken poison. My daughter in law then left the premises to ring the police. I put the lysol bottle in the chest of drawers, away from the children. Constable Piggott arrived later and asked me if the deceased David Walker had taken lysol and I told him he had not. I was so confused I forgot to tell Mr Piggott that I broke up the cup and put it in the dust bin and wiped up the vomit. Deceased was sitting on the side of the bed when Mr Piggott came in. He said to deceased. Have you taken any lysol, and deceased said NO. He also asked me if he had drunk any of the wine and deceased said Yes. Mr Piggott found the lysol bottle in the chest of drawers. Mr Piggott smelt the cups in the room and smelt deceased's breath and looked in his mouth. Mr Piggott then said to deceased, Come on, Come on Dave you will have to leave the house. The deceased was stubborn but Mr Piggott coaxed him out. The bottle produced similar to the one that deceased took from his pocket.

Signed Sarah Waters.

Deposition of a Witness

This Deponent, Lavinia May Garlepp

On her oath saith, I am a married woman residing at 121 Station Street, Port Melbourne.

The deceased David Alexander Walker was known to me for the last seven years. About 8.30 a.m. on the 3rd day of September, 1935 I left my home leaving my mother in law, Saran Ann Walker in the house. About 10.30 o'clock the same morning I returned to my home and immediately went out again and returned about fifteen minutes later and saw the deceased sitting in my mother in laws bed.

He appeared to be intoxicated and did not speak to me, neither did I speak to him. My mother in law said I think Dave has taken poison. I detected a smell of lysol and rang the Port Melbourne Police Station and asked for Mr Piggott to sent to 121 Station Street, at once. I did not see any lysol in the room, or vomit. The deceased did not make any complaint about having taken poison. Mr Piggott arrived afterwards and asked me what I wanted him for and I told him that my mother in law thought Dave Walker who was inside had taken lysol. Mr Piggott entered the front room whilst I went to into the back of the premises. I was not present in the room where Mr Piggott was with the deceased and my mother in law. Later I asked Mr Piggott to remove the deceased from my house as I did not want him there when my husband came home. I have had to get the police on two previous occasions owing to the deceased's behaviour whilst under the influence of liquor. I always resented him coming to my home.

Signed   Lavinia May Garlepp

MAN AND YOUTH FOR TRIAL ON MURDER CHARGES

After an inquest yesterday into the death of Walter Edward Copley, 28, of Somerset, England, cabin steward on the P and O liner *Strathmore*, Mr Marwick, city coroner, committed a man and a youth for trial on charges of murder.

Mr Marwick found that Copley had died from skull fractures, brain lacerations, and hemorrhage, in Prince Henry's Hospital on October 7. His death had been caused by injuries inflicted the previous day in a garden plantation near North Port railway station by Reginald William Watson, 28, labourer, of Cecil st, South Melbourne, and Donald Joseph Walker, 15½, labourer, of Gladstone st, Montague. Applications for bail were refused.

Detective-Sergeant Halsall, CIB homicide squad, said in evidence that Watson and Walker told him they had intended to rob Copley. Witness read a statement by Watson, in which he said he had hit Copley with his fist, and that Walker was not in the plantation with him at the time.

On 27 October, 1945, the Argus reported that Donald Joseph Walker, Viiolet and David's 15 year old son had been charged with murder.

On 28 November, 1945 the Herald reported that the charges had been withdrawn.

Murder Charge Withdrawn

The Prosecutor for the King (Mr Leo Little) announced in the Criminal Court today that the Attorney-General had entered a nolle prosequi in the case in which Donald Joseph Walker of Gladstone Street, South Melbourne, had been committed for trial by the Coroner (Mr Marwick PM) on a charge of having murdered Walter Edward Copley, cabin steward, who had been a member of the crew of the Strathmore.

Walker would be arrested on another charge when he left the Court, Mr Little added.

Reginald William Watson, of Cecil Street, South Melbourne builders laborer who had pleaded guilty to the manslaughter of Copley was remanded for sentence by Mr Justice O'Bryan. He admitted convictions for larceny, unlawful wounding and minor offences.

Evidence was given at the inquest that Copley had been attacked with a bottle in a plantation near North Port railway station on the night of October 6.

Wilhelm (William) Garlepp descendants

married	1885
Sarah Ann French	1867-1935
children	
Mary Agnes French/Garlepp	1884–1951
married	1906
John Edward Buckley	1876–1959
children	
Thomas James Buckley	1909–1959
John Edward Buckley Jr	1911–1980
Earnest William Kenneth Buckley	1911–1979
Unknown	
children	
John Patrick Garlepp	1920–1984
Elizabeth Anistasia Garlepp	1886–1886
William George Garlepp	1887–1964
married	1908
Alma Veronica Neenan	1890-1949
children	
William Austin Garlepp	1908–1982
married	1938
Gladys Elizabeth Moffatt	1912–1995
children	
Janice Ann Garlepp	1939–2018
Sharon Garlepp	??
Ernest John Garlepp	1909–1993
married	1936
Gladys Mary McLennan	1917–1981
children	
Thelma Garlepp	1936–1936
married	1954
Burnie Elizabeth Connelly	1909–1997
Alice Veronika Garlepp	1912–1998
Married	1931
Horace Charles Rosewarne	1908–1995
Children	
Thomas Charles Rosewarne	1935–2008
Nellie Murial Olive Garlepp	1913–1988
Freda Violet Myrtle Garlepp	1918–1998
married	1951
Reuben Matthew Morrissey	

Kathleen Alma Garlepp		1922-
married		1945
Leslie Ralph McCole		1920–
children		
Robyn Lesliegh McCole		1949–2007
Barrie Ronald McCole		–1994
Lillian May Garlepp		1924–1995
married		1943
Brandon Joseph Fox		1922–2000
married		1949
Kenneth Raymond Kiely		1920–1985
children		
Charman Kiely		
Christine Kiely		
Glen Kiely		
Cheryl Kiely		
John Joseph Garlepp		1927–1957
Thomas George Garlepp		1928-1999
married		1949
Thelma Irene Halliday		1910-2007
Robert Morris (Bob) Garlepp		1931-2023
marrled		1954
Mary Thelma Anderson		1930–2019
children		
Colleen Maree Garlepp		1956–2013
Brendan Garlepp		
Wayne Garlepp		
Brett Garlepp		
Pam Garlepp		
John Garlepp		
Coral Lorraine Garlepp		??
Ernest Edward Garlepp		1891–1971
married		1929
Lavinia Craker		1894-1939
Sarah Ann Garlepp		1893–1980
married		1915
Edward John Amy		1892–1969
children		
Edward John Verdun Amy		1916–1987
John Thomas Amy		1920–1924

Violet Lily Myrtle Garlepp	1898–
married	1917
James William Eldridge	1879–1978
Children	
Iris Myra Kathleen Eldridge	1918–1978
Agnes Myrtle Eldridge Waters	1921–1921
married	1922
David Alexander Walker	1887–1935
children	
Leslie Walker	1924–
Cyril Alexander Walker	1924–1924
Daniel Joseph Walker	1927–1927
John Walker	1929–
Donald Joseph Walker	1930–2020
Lillian Walker	1934–

Hermann Garlepp

Hermann Garlepp was born in 1859 in Melbourne. He was the first of the family to be born in Australia after his parents and older brothers arrived in 1856.

Hermann never married. He was a farmer in the Lima area of Victoria. He had 320 acres which he sold in 1893. According to the electoral rolls he called himself a labourer. I'm assuming this was farm labour.

BENALLA LAND BOARD.

Messrs Thomas and Dunn, land officers, presided on Tuesday last, when the following applications were

RECOMMENDED.

James S. Lamont, Boho, 160a
George Bullock, Boomahnoomoonha, 220a
Thomas Bullock, Boomahnoomoonah, 298a
Patrick Brady, 14, sec 4, Branjee, 320a
John Artridge, 18, sec 4, Branjee, 320a
Charlotte A. Worland, 18, sec 4, Branjee, 320a
John Hammer, Branjee, 107a
William Worland, 14, sec 4, Branjee, 143a
Johanna Lonergan, 15, sec 4, Branjee, 320a
William Archer, 103, 104, Goomalibee, 320a
John Archer, 105, 106, Goomalibee, 320a
Patrick Kelly, pt 58, Goomalibee, 43a
Mary H. Davies, 82, 93, Goomalibee, 320a
Henry Davies, pt 103, 104, 95, Goomalibee, 320a
Henry Wilson, pt 92, 56, Goomalibee, 320a
Alfred G. Avery, Gooramgooramgong, 93a
Thomas Gardner, Gooramgooramgong, 175a
William Wilson, Gowangardie, 197a
James Hogan, pt 24, 25, Gowangardie, 50a
Mary Coffey, pt 24, 25, Gowangardie, 86a—For about 30 acres
Herman Garlepp, Lima, 320a
John Garlepp, Lima, 320a
William A. Higgins, 87, Mokoan, 142a
Joseph Harrison, pt 34, 35, Moorngag, 132a
John Walker, pt 25, Moorngag, 65a (non residence)
George Humphrey, Strathbogie, 100a
Robert Cumming, Tatong, 53a
James Holden, Tatong, 254a
Abraham Holden, Tatong, 41a
Edward Cain, Tatong, 193a
Duncan M'Ivor, Tatong, 177a
Michael Ryan, Tatong, 100a
John Fairley, Tharanbegga, 70a—Subject to payment of valuation for improvements
Benjamin Marshall, Toombullup, 70a
James Plozza, pt 7, 8, Upotipotpon, 320a
John G. West, pt 18, 19, Upotipotpon, 320a
Henry L. Angus, pt 12, Upotipotpon, 320a
Patrick O'Sullivan, senr., pt 28, 28, Upotipotpon, 85a
George Webb, pt 50, 51, Upotipotpon, 320a
George Webb, pt 50, 51, Upotipotpon, 320a
William Ryan, pt 44, Upotipotpon, 160a
Annie M'Louglin, 8, Upotipotpon, 320a
Joseph Pethybridge, 14, Upotipotpon, 320a
Andrew Black, 33, Upotipotpon, 320a
John Johns, Waggarandall, 18a
Alexander Leggat, Warrenbayne, 162a
Mary Jane Farrin, pt 41, Warrenbayne, 120a
Harriett Wilson, 41, 42, Warrenbayne, 320a—Subject to survey
William Fowler, pt 77, Winton, 120a
Samuel Dodemaide, Yabba Yabba, 160a—For 47a 0r 15p
Patrick Treacy, Yabba Yabba, 160a —For 50 acres
William Payne, Yabba Yabba, 160a —For part of southern portion
Henry Warfe, Yabba Yabba, 160a —For part of southern portion

RE-HEARING.

Thomas Herridge, Waggarandall, 216a—Recommended
Robert Ralston, Moglonemby, 200a
C. O'C. Meagher, Moglonemby, 200a
Bridget Daly, Moglonemby, 200a
John Broderick, Moglonemby, 72a
These four were rival applicants. The board's former decision was upheld in this instance, the land being recommended to Ralston, a farm laborer, single, residing at Faithful's Creek

REFUSED.

Robert Murray, Boho, 160a
Michael Connors, 15, sec 4, Branjee, 320a
George G. Gardner, Gooramgooramgong, 175a
Lachlan D. Grant, 33, Upotipotpon, 320a
Angus M'Cormick, 33, Upotipotpon, 320a
Michael Flaherty, 33, Upotipotpon, 320a
Stephen Milne, Yabba Yabba, 160a
John Brown, Yabba Yabba, 160a
Charles Heal, Yabba Yabba, 160a
Frederick Potzsch, Yabba Yabba, 160a
John O'Connor, Yabba Yabba, 80a
Laurence Gleeson, Yabba Yabba, 160a
James Keogh, Yabba Yabba, 160a
Thomas Kilburn, Yabba Yabba, 160a

POSTPONED.

Laura L. Down, 111, 112, Goomalibee, 320a
Donald M'Larty, 16, Goomalibee, 320a
Patrick Kildea, Gowangardie, 320a
William Bush, junr., Strathbogie, 320a
Kenneth M'Ivor, junr., Tatong, 320a

A notice in the North Eastern Ensign on 27 June 1884 states that Herman's application for 320 acres in Lima was recommended.

The newspaper article below is from the
North Eastern Ensign 15 August 1884

GAZETTE NOTICES

A site of 4 acres, being part of al.
lotment 113a, parish of Glenrowan,
has been reserved for quarrying purposes.

Five acres, part of allotment 53,
parish of Tatong, have been reserved
for State-school purposes.

Applications for licenses approved
—H. L. Angus, P. O'Sullivan, senr.,
James Plozza, George Webb, Mary
Looby, Geo. Golding, Thomas Ma-
guire, Upotipotpon ; John Archer, H.
Davies, Mary H. Davies, H. Wilson,
D. Kenneally junr., Thomas Carey,
Patrick Carey, M. Keneally, D. Davies,
Goomalibee ; Wm. Clark, John and
Herman Garlepp, Lima ; F. Hum
phrey, Strathbogie ; Wm. Fowler,
Winton ; Thomas Gardner, Gooram ;
Duncan M'Ivor, Tatong ; Joseph Har-
rison, Henry Dennis, M. A. Evans,
John Walker, Moorngag ; J. S.

The article to the
right and finishing
below an article in
North Eastern Ensign
on 21 February 1893

I have transcribed it
on the following
page.

Michael Farrell stated :—I know the
property bought by the plaintiff. I was
in possession of the land till the end of
August last, when I gave it up to the
defendant. My lease expired on the
1st of October. I paid Garlepp £1 a
month for the use of the land from the
10th of July to the 1st October.

This was the case for the plaintiff.

Defendant said :—I got the agreement produced from Herman Garlepp.
By that agreement he gave me the
use of his land at £1 per month for 12
months.

To Mr Vasey—I took possession of
the land on the day after I made the
agreement with Garlepp, and remained
there for about two months. I received
a letter from Lamrock, Brown and
Hall telling me to take my sheep off
the land. I did not take them off then,
but I afterwards removed them for a
few days as I wanted to shear them. I
pay £12 a year for the grass.

Mr Vasey contended that the agreement between Smith and Garlepp was
useless as it had not been registered.

His Honor thought differently, however, and said—Well, I think the
parties might settle it between themselves.

Mr Ryan—Well, I was willing to
settle it.

His Honor—All right, off you go and
settle it. I can do nothing for you.

Smith.—But is my agreement any
good, your Honor ?

His Honor—Yes, good enough as
far as I can see.

The plaintiff was consequently non-
suited without costs.

RYAN V. SMITH.

This was a claim for £49—damages
for trespass.

Mr Vasey (instructed by Mr T.
Brown) appeared for the plaintiff, the
defendant conducting his own case.

Mr Vasey stated that the plaintiff
had purchased some land in Lima from
the National Bank, which institution
held it under mortgage, the mortgagee
being Herman Garlepp. Since purchase of the land the defendant's sheep
had trespassed on the property and done
damage to the extent of the amount
claimed.

The defendant, by way of defense,
denied the trespass, stating that he
was legally in possession of the land
under an agreement between the mortgagee and himself.

Edward Ryan said :—I know the
land in question. I bought it from
Herman Garlepp, it being at that time
under mortgage. I paid the mortgage
off to the National Bank in September
last. I took possession on the 12th
October. John Garlepp and Peter
Murray were present. The paddocks
contained 320 acres. I placed a man
named John Garlepp in possession. In
November I sent wire to land for fencing. In consequence of what I heard
I had a letter sent to defendant asking
him to take his sheep off my land. In
February I went out to the land and
saw some of defendant's sheep there.
There were about 300 sheep there, I
think. I think my loss has been about
1s an acre. That is £16.

His Honor—But the claim is £49.

Samuel Kitson said : —I am manager
of the National Bank, Benalla. I know
that plaintiff bought Garlepp's land
from the Bank.

John Garlepp stated :—I am a farmer
residing at Lima. I know the property
in question. I saw defendant's sheep
on the land in January. Plaintiff gave
me charge of the place. The sheep
were on the land from the 18th January
to the 9th of February. They were in
a paddock of 240 acres. I think the

damage done to the land would be
covered by about 1s per acre. On the
2nd of November I sent defendant
note telling him he was not to put his
sheep in the paddock.

To defendant—1s an acre is as near
as I can guess to the damage done to
the land by the trespass of your sheep.

Andrew Jenson said : —I know the
land in question. I saw defendant's
sheep on the land in February. I saw
about 300 or 400 sheep there.

100

RYAN V. SMITH. This was a claim for £49-damages for trespass. Mr Vasey (instructed by Mr T. Brown) appeared for the plaintiff, the defendant conducting his own case.

Mr Vasey stated that the plaintiff had purchased some land in Lima from the National Bank, which institution held it under mortgage, the mortgagee being Herman Garlepp. Since purchase of the land the defendant's sheep had trespassed on the property and done damage to the extent of the amount claimed. The defendant, by way of defence, denied, the trespass, stating that he was legally in possession of the land under an agreement between the mortgagee and himself.

Edward Ryan said :- I know the land in question. I bought it from Herman Garlepp, it being at that time under mortgage. I paid the mortgage off to the National Bank in September last. I took possession on the 12th October. John Garlepp and Pete Murray were present. The paddocks contained 320 acres. I placed a man named John Garlepp in possession. In November I sent wire to land for fencing. In consequence of what I heard I had a letter sent to defendant asking him take his sheep off my land. In February I went out to the land and saw some of defendant's sheep there. There were about 200 sheep there, I think. I think my loss has been about 1s an acre. That is £16.

His Honor--But the claim is £49. but Samuel Kitson said:--I am manager of the National Bank, Benalla, I know that plaintiff bought Garlepp's land from the Bank.

John Garlepp stated :- I am a farmer residing in Lima. I know the property in question. I saw defendant's sheep on the land in January. Plaintiff gave me charge of the place. The sheep were on the land from the 18th January to the 9th February. They were in a paddock of 240 acres. I think the damage done to the land would be covered by about 1s per acre. On the 2nd of November I sent defendant a note telling him he was not to put his sheep in the paddock.

To defendant   1s an acre is as near as I can guess to the damage done to the land by the trespass of your sheep.

Andrew Jenson said :- I know the land in question. I saw defendant's sheep on the land in February. I saw about 300 or 400 sheep there.

Michael Farrell stated:- I know the property bought by the plaintiff. I was in possession of the land till the end of August last, when I gave it up on to the defendant. My lease expired on the 1st of October. I paid Garlepp 1 pound a month for the use of the land from the 10th of July to the 1st October. This was the case for the plaintiff.

Defendant said:- I got the agreement produced from Herman Garlepp. By that agreement he gave me the use of his land at £1 per month for 12 months.

To Mr Vasey - I took possession of the land on the day after I made the agreement with Garlepp and remained there for about two months. I received a letter from Lamrock, Brown and Hall telling me to take my sheep off the land. I did not take them off then, but I afterwards removed them for a few days as I wanted to shear them. I pay £12 a year for the grass.

Mr Vasey contended that the agreement between Smith and Garlepp was useless as it had not been registered.

His Honor thought differently, how ever, and said - Well I think the parties might settle it between them selves.

Mr. Ryan - Well I was willing to settle it. His Honor - All right, off you go and settle it. I can do nothing for you.

Smith:- But is my agreement any good your Honor?

His Honor-- Yes, good enough as far as I can see. The plaintiff was consequently non-suited without cost.

Hermann found a huge snake in the paddock. The Benalla Standard reported about this on 15 October, 1926.

LIMA EAST.

One of the largest brown snakes killed in this district for many years was accounted for by Hermann Garlepp, in Mr. V. Heaney's paddock on Saturday last. It measured 6ft 5in. Two more, 3ft 6in, were killed the next day at the same spot.

MR H. GARLEPP.

The death occurred on Saturday morning in Wangaratta, of an old age pensioner named Mr Herman Garlepp, who resided in the Lima East district. He was 73 years of age. The funeral took place to the Wangaratta cemetery on Monday. Canon Wray read the burial service and Irving's Pty. Ltd. carried out arrangements.

Herman died in September, 1931.

He was 73 years old and was buried in the Wangaratta cemetery.

Hermann died intestate as the article in the Benalla Standard, 19 January, 1932 says. (right)

NOTICE.—A Rule to administer the Estate of HERMAN GARLEPP, late of Lima, near Benalla, laborer, deceased, intestate, who died on the 2nd September, 1931, has been granted to me, and Creditors, Next of Kin, and all others having CLAIMS against the estate are required to SEND IN PARTICULARS of their claims to the Curator of the Estates of Deceased Persons, No. 267 Queen Street, Melbourne, on or before the 22nd March, 1932, or they may be excluded from the distribution of the estate when the assets are being distributed.

Heinrich Garlepp (Henry)

Heinrich Garlepp, or as he was later called, Henry, was born in 1861 in the Craigieburn area of Victoria. He was the seventh son of Charles and Elizabeth Garlepp.

In 1884 he was fined in the Violet Town court, for burning timber on crown land.

On 27 May, 1886, in Benalla Victoria, when Henry was 25, he married Catherine (Kate) French (1858-1925). Kate was the daughter of John French (1833-1917) and Ellen O'Halloran (1833-1903). Kate was also the sister of Ellen and Sarah Ann French who also married into the Garlepp family.

They lived in the Violet Town area where their daughter, Ellen (1887-1942) was born.

In 1888 Henry was fined for Insulting Behaviour in a public place. Shortly following this, Henry, Kate and Ellen moved to Port Melbourne.

On 26 February, 1889 their second daughter was born. Kathleen (1889-1956) was baptised on 26 May, 1889 in Port Melbourne.

According to the Rate Books, Henry was renting a 2 bedroom wooden house in Port Melbourne in 1891.

On 8 May, 1891, George Patrick (1891-1954) was born. He was baptised 4 July, 1891 in Port Melbourne.

In 1894 Mary was born. Unfortunately she also died the same year. Her death is registered as 2 January, 1894.

According to the City Directory, the family had moved to 11 Clifford Street, Port Melbourne and remained here for a few years.

In 1898 another daughter was born. Agnes (1898-1961). The birth was registered as Heathcote, which is interesting.

Here is a picture of early Port Melbourne. I found it...

Arthur Hester – Port Melbourne Historical and Preservation Society (pmhps.org.au)

In 1900, Henry applied for a Voter's Certificate. It was the time of Federation and every eligible person was required to get themselves onto the Electoral Roll. The application was made in the Hawthorn court, where they had moved to.

In 1901 Henry and Kate had another child, Edward (1901-1931).

In 1903 Henry was fined for not sending Henry junior and George to school.

In 1904 the family are living at 7 Lynch Street, Hawthorn. Henry is again fined for not sending Henry Junior to school.

In 1908, the family were living at 25 Camberwell Road, Hawthorn.

Henry's occupation was usually cited as being a labourer.

Henry died suddenly on 26 October, 1916 at the age of 55. According to the notices below, found in The Age, the family were living at 183 Camberwell Road, Upper Hawthorn at the time. Henry was buried in the Box Hill Cemetery.

GARLEPP.—On the 19th October, at 183 Camberwell-road, Henry, the dearly beloved husband of Kate Garlepp, and father Mrs. Harnden, Mrs. Little, George, Henry, Molly, Edward, and son-in-law of John French, beloved brother-in-law of Mrs. Waters and Mrs. Nelson, of Port Melbourne, aged 55 years.
Nearer, my God, to Thee.

GARLEPP.—On the 19th October (suddenly), at his residence, 183 Camberwell road, Upper Hawthorn, Henry, the beloved husband of Catherine Garlepp, and beloved father of Mrs. J. Harnden, Mr. James Little, jun.; George, Henry, Agnes and Edward, aged 55 years. R.I.P.

GARLEPP.—The Friends of Mrs. CATHERINE GARLEPP are respectfully invited to follow the remains of her beloved husband, Henry, to the place of interment, in the Box Hill Cemetery. The funeral will leave his residence, 183 Camberwell-road, Upper Hawthorn, THIS DAY (Saturday), 21st October, at 3 p.m.
FREDE and SONS, Undertakers, 380 Burwood road, Glenferrie. Telephones: 7, Hawthorn Ex.; 347, Canterbury Ex.

Catherine died 21 June, 1925. A notice was placed in the Age on 22 June 1925

GARLEPP.—On the 21st June, at 200 Camberwell-road, Upper Hawthorn, Catherine, relict of the late Henry Garlepp, and loving mother of Ellen (Mrs. J. Harnden), Kate (Mrs. J. Little), George, Henry, Mollie and Edward, aged 65 years.
R.I.P.

Ellen Garlepp, Henry and Kate's eldest child was born in Violet Town in 1887. In 1907 she married James Spencer Harnden (1884-1972) in Melbourne. James was born in Melbourne and was the son of Henry Collin Harnden (1855-1894) and Mary Jane Thornton (1862-1915).

Ellen and James lived at 8 Rose Street, Auburn until about 1819 and then they moved to 59 Edgar Street, Footscray North. The picture to the right is a modern look at the Rose Street house.

James occupation was given as Labourer.

Ellen and James had the following children

Edward Harnden	1924–1999
Ellen Mary Harnden	1926–2002
Patricia Nancy Harnden	1928–2013
Ernest Spencer Harnden	1930–2016

HARNDEN.—On May 29, at her resi-
dence, 59 Edgar-street, West Footscray,
Ellen, the dearly beloved wife of James
Spencer Harnden, loving mother of Kathleen
(Mrs. R. Whitten), Jimmy, Bill (de-
ceased), Agnes (Mrs. A. Strong), George,
Harry, Jack, Ned, Nellie, Patsy and Ernie,
beloved mother-in-law of Bessie (Mrs. J.
Harnden), Norreen (Mrs. G. Harnden), aged
54 years.   R.I.P.
HAY.—On May 31, John Wilson loving

Ellen died 29 may, 1942 at 54 years of age.

The article to the left was published in The Age on 1 June 1942.

James died 19 April, 1972.

The are buried in the Footscray Cemetery

Kathleen Garlepp was the second child of Henry and Kate. She was born 26 February, 1889 and was baptised in Port Melbourne on 28 May 1889.

In 1910 Kathleen married James William Little (1892-1964) James was the son of James Little (1863–1937) and Anna Maria Roff {1867–1945)

Kathleen and James had the following children:

James William Henry Little	1911–1952
Nellie Veneta Little	1912–1982

Kathleen died in 1956 and James died in 1964.

George Patrick Garlepp was the third child of Henry and Kate. He was born 8 May 1891 Port Melbourne. He was baptised 4 July, 1891.

When George was about 23 he found himself the topic of the news. The first news article appeared on 12 April, 1913 in the Herald. I have transcribed it below. Over the next few pages I have included a number of articles that talk about this story.

From the articles we can disseminate a lot of information. We find out about George and Grace's relationship with each other and her parents. We find that there is a child stillborn (Edith May Garlepp 1914 -1914) before their marriage. We find out Grace's residences during the period talked about, including "The Haven" which was an institution run by the Salvation Army. I will discuss this later in this chapter because it's an interesting story as well.

I find the story very sad, but has a positive outcome.

Alleged Abduction
Young Man Arrested

On April 2, 1912, a girl named Grace Shore disappeared from her parents home and Council Street, Auburn. Nothing was heard of the girl by her family until last week, when the police discovered her at Fitzroy. In consequence of information given by the girl, Plains clothes constables Coughlin and Burke and Constable Goodyer of Hawthorn went to Redfern Road, Auburn last night and arrested a man named George Garlepp aged 22 on a charge of abduction.

Garlepp was charged at the Hawthorn Court this morning, before Mr W Morrison, JP and the case was remanded until Tuesday. Bail was allowed in assurety of one hundred pounds and Garlepp's bond for a like amount.

ALLEGED ABDUCTION

YOUNG MAN ARRESTED

On April 2, 1912, a girl named Grace Shore disappeared from her parents' home at Council street, Auburn. Nothing was heard of the girl by her friends until last week, when the police discovered her at Fitzroy. In consequence of information given by the girl, plain clothes-constables Coughlin and Burke and Constable Goodyer, of Hawthorn, went to Redfern road, Auburn, last night and arrested a man named George Garlitt aged 22 on a charge of abduction.

Garlitt was charged at the Hawthorn Court this morning, before Mr W Morrison, J P, and the case was remanded until Tuesday. Bail was allowed in one surety of £100 and Garlitt's bond for a like amount.

The story continued in the Argus 16 April 1913 (Transcribed below)

Girls Infatuation. Police Court Case
George Garlepp aged about 23 years, was charged at the Hawthorn Court on Tuesda with having taken into his possession against the will of her father. Grace Louise Shore, a girl under 18 years of age.
Sub inspector Keegan prosecuted and Mr E J Carr defended.
Evidence was given by Grace Shore that she met Garlepp two years ago, and kept company with him. In April, 1911 she went away with him to Port Melbourne and then to Williamstown, where she obtained employment as a domestic servant. He visited her frequently. He then took her to a boarding-house in Fitzroy, and left her. She was taken from there to the Salvation Army Home at North Fitzroy.
Under cross examination she admitted being very fond of Garlepp and asked him to take her away. When he refused she ran away from home, and Garlepp found her.
Sydney Shore, father of the girl said that the girl went away contrary to his wishes. She was of weak intellect and he would not consent to her marriage with Garlepp.
Mr Carr said that the girl had become infatuated with Garlepp and had followed him everywhere. She asked him to take her away.
The case was dismissed.

GIRL'S INFATUATION.

POLICE COURT CASE.

George Garlipp, aged about 23 years, was charged at the Hawthorn Court on Tuesday with having taken into his possession, against the will of her father, Grace Louisa Shore, a girl under 18 years of age.

Sub-inspector Keegan prosecuted, and Mr E. J. Corr defended.

Evidence was given by Grace Shore that she met Garlipp two years ago, and kept company with him. In April, 1911, she went away with him to Port Melbourne, and then to Williamstown, where she obtained employment as a domestic servant. He visited her frequently. He then took her to a boardinghouse in Fitzroy, and left her. She was taken from there to the Salvation Army Home at North Fitzroy.

Under cross-examination, she admitted being very fond of Garlipp, and had asked him to take her away. When he refused she ran away from home, and Garlipp found her.

Sydney Shore, father of the girl, said that the girl went away contrary to his wishes. She was of weak intellect, and he would not consent to her marriage with Garlipp.

Mr Corr said that the girl had become infatuated with Garlipp, and had followed him everywhere. She asked him to take her away.

The case was dismissed.

CHARGE OF ABDUCTION.

A PITIFUL STORY.

The Hawthorn court yesterday was packed to the doors during the hearing of a charge against George Garbtt, a young labourer, of "having taken Grace Shore, aged 17, out of the possession of her father and without his consent, with intent." Messrs. Philpott, Dallas and Roche, J's.P., constituted the bench. Mr. Corr appeared for the defence, and Inspector Keegan for the prosecution.

Mr. Corr considered that the matter might be settled by the marriage of the parties, and asked for an adjournment with this object.

Inspector Keegan said the matter had got too far for that.

Grace Shore, who was suffering so severely from nervous prostration that she was accommodated with a seat on the floor of the court, gave her evidence in a most contradictory way. She stated she had left her parents in Auburn "on her own," because she was unhappy. She had been intimate with accused before she ran away. She went into domestic service at Williamstown, where accused visited her every week. When the state of her health required that she should lay up, accused took her to lodgings at Fitzroy, and after seeing her once never came back again. She then went to the Salvation Army haven in North Fitzroy, where she had a baby, which had since died. Previous to running away finally, she had left her home, but accused induced her to return. Next morning she ran away altogether. She went to accused's home at 7 a.m., knocked at his window, told him she was running away, and asked him to go with her. Accused refused, and tried to get her to return home. She then went away without accused knowing where she was going. Subsequently accused found her. Continuing, witness said: "I am very fond of George himself, and would have married him if my father and mother would have consented. I am still fond of him, and am willing to marry him now. He never induced me to go away."

Sydney George Shore said that Grace Shore was his daughter. She was 17 years of age last January. He had caught her with accused one night and gave her two cuts with a cane and told her to go home. She did not go home, and at 1 a.m. witness and Constable Dunne found her with accused in the street. He took her home, and next morning she ran away. His daughter was "deficient," and he had told accused "she was no fit girl for him to run after."

To the Chairman: He would not let her marry accused. Grace was infatuated with the man.

Annie Shore, mother of Grace, gave similar evidence. After her daughter had run away accused called at her house in a state of intoxication and said he wanted to marry Grace. Witness replied, "I would rather see her put through a mincing machine." Subsequently accused called again, told her Grace was in a certain condition and asked permission to marry her. Witness again refused, saying it was too late now. Accused refused to say where Grace was at that time.

Constable Dunne gave evidence that when he found the girl at 1 a.m. a day or so before she ran away she was with accused and accused's sister. When witness asked accused why he was with the girl at that hour in the morning he replied that her father and mother were very cruel to her; that her mother had knocked her down and dragged her up a right of way by the hair. He (accused) and his sister had taken her to Camberwell police station, as she refused to go home, and as they could not make anyone hear they were taking her to Auburn police station, hoping to find someone in charge of it.

Evidence was also given that when accused took the girl to Fitzroy he paid only 9/ for her lodgings, and that the landlady kept her for three weeks out of charity until she was handed over to the Salvation Army.

The Chairman said accused had behaved shamefully to the girl, and had proved himself a confirmed scamp. However, there was no evidence that accused had taken the girl away and the case would be dismissed. Accused was then discharged.

This article was in the Age on 16 April 1913

The transcription is on the following page.

CHARGE OF ABDUCTION.

A PITIFUL STORY

The Hawthorn court yesterday was packed to the doors during the hearing of a charge against George Garlepp, a young labourer, of having "taken Grace Shore, aged 17, out of the possession of her father and without his consent, with intent". Messrs. Philpott,, Duffus and Roche, JPs., constituted the bench. Mr Carr appeared for the defence, and Inspector Keegan for the prosecution. Mr. Carr considered that the matter might be settled by the marriage of the parties, and asked for an adjournment with this object. Inspector Keegan said the matter had got too far for that.

Grace Shore, who was suffering so severely from nervous prostration that she was accommodated with a seat on the floor of the court, gave her evidence in a most contradictory way. She stated she had left her parents in Auburn "on her own" because she was unhappy. She had been intimate with accused before she ran away. She went io domestic service at Williamstown, where accused visited her every week. When the state of her health required that she should lay up, accused took her to lodgings at Fitzroy, and after seeing her once never came back again. She then went to the Salvation Army haven in North Fitzroy, where she had a baby, which had since died. Previous to running away finally, she had left her home, but accused induced her to return. Next morning she ran away altogether. She went to accused's house ul 7 a.m., knocked at it's window, told him she was running away, and asked him to go with her. Accused refused, and tried to get her to return home. She then went away with out accused knowing where she was going. Subsequently accused found her. Continuing witness said: "I am very fond of George (accused), and would have married him if my father and mother would have consented. I am still fond of him, and am willing to marry him now. He never induced me to go away."
Sydney George Shore said that Grace Shore was his daughter. She was 17 years of age last January. He had caught her with accused one night and gave her two cuts with a cane and told her to go home. She did not go home, and at 1 a.m. witness and Constable Dunne found her with accused in the street. He took her home, and next morning she ran away. His daughter was "deficient" and he had told accused "she was no fit girl for him to run after"

To the Chairman: He would not let her marry accused. Grace was infatuated with the man.

.

Annie Shore, mother of Grace, gave simi lar evidence. After her daughter had run away accused called at her house in a state of intoxication and said he wanted to marry Grace. Witness replied, "I would rather see her put through a mincing machine". Subsequently accused called again, told her Grace was in a certain condition and asked permission to marry her. Witness again refused, saying it was too late now. Accused refused to say where Grace was at that time.

Constable Dunne gave evidence that when he found the girl at 1 a.m. a day or so before she ran away she was with accused and accused's sister. When witness asked accused why he was with the girl at that hour in the morning he replied that her father and mother were very cruel to her; that her mother had knocked her down and dragged her up a right of way by the hair. He (accused) and his sister had taken her to Camberwell police station, as she refused to home, and as they could not make anyone hear they were taking her to Auburn police station, hoping to find someone in charge of it.

Evidence was also given that when accused took the girl to Fitzroy he paid only 9/ for her lodgings, and that the landlady kept her for three weeks out of charity until she was handed over to the Salvation Army.

The Chairman said accused had behaved shamefully to the girl, and had proved him self a confirmed scamp. However, there was no evidence that accused had taken the girl away and the case would be dismissed. Accused was then discharged

In the Box Hill Reporter on 18 April, 1913, there was another article about the case.

I have transcribed it over the next couple of pages, for easier readability.

HAWTHORN POLICE COURT.

Tuesday, April 15

The duties of adjudication were carried out by Mr. Philpott (chairman), and Messrs. Roche, Duffus, Wallis, Henningsen and Ardagh, J's.P.

Immigrant's Shocking Behavior

Walter James Briggs was charged with having behaved indecently on Saturday, April 12. Accused pleaded guilty. Constable Mahoney stated at about 4 p.m. he saw accused in the West Hawthorn gardens, and proceeded to give evidence in support of the charge. A number of women and little girls were about. It was a wilful action. Arthur Rowe, clerk, corroborated. To Sub-inspector Keegan. There is no doubt but that his behavior was wilful. I watched him for some time. Accused: I have nothing to say. Sub-inspector Keegan. I understand he is one of the immigrants. Accused (to Sergeant Mumford): Yes, I am a true Englishman. I paid my own way out. Constable Mahoney: I understand he has been out here for 12 months. Mr. Henningsen: If that's the class of person they send out here Heaven help the country.

The chairman: This is simply the act of a perfect lunatic. The bench is getting tired of this sort of thing. This man does not seem to feel his position either. He rather seems to glory in it. In my opinion a man guilty of such conduct ought to be incarcerated permanently. We can understand a man picking another man's pocket; he goes for money; but here it is mere vice and with no other object than the gratification of vice. Is there no way that such a man can be dealt with ... quite content as it is, and when he is liberated again he will go into a public park again and misbehave himself again. The Sub-inspector: The most any of us can say is that he is not fit to be at large. The chairman: If he came out here to serve his country the only service he has done to the land of his nativity is by leaving it.

Accused was sentenced to 12 months' imprisonment with hard labor. The chairman said some of the justices did not care to go further, but two years would be little enough. If accused was not right no doubt the authorities would see what was the proper place for him.

The Troubles of William Slack

William Slack was charged on bail with having been drunk on Saturday, 12th inst. Constable Kennedy said on 6.30 p.m. accused was making a perfect nuisance of himself outside the town hall when in a drunken condition. Sergeant Mumford: He is a very old client of ours. He has already paid £1 this year. Accused: By —, I would like to have as many thousand. The chairman: Be quiet; you want a whole court house for yourself. Accused: The constable came behind me in the crowd and caught me by the throat. The chairman: Did he hurt you? Accused: Of course he hurt me. But if you hit them it means a tenner. Sergeant Mumford: There are convictions against him, mostly for drunkenness and offensive behavior. He is all right when not drinking. Accused was fined £5, in default one month's gaol. Accused: You will have me leaving the town with a swag on my back next. There you are. Accused was allowed 7 days in which to pay the fine.

Motor Collides With Cart

Chauffeur Fined.

John Hunter was charged with, on March 22, having driven a motor car at a speed dangerous to the public. Defendant pleaded not guilty. Mr. Carroll appeared for defendant. Joseph Henry Quincey, sawdust merchant, Noon street, Clifton Hill, said he was driving across Burwood road at the intersection of Auburn road. He saw a motor car about 40 yards down the road. Suddenly he felt a bump at the back of the car. He was nearly ... damaged. Then the ... into the car and drive off. He took no notice of his hail, but made off. He took the number of the car. Defendant was travelling at about 20 to 24 miles an hour; he was on a down grade. A bag of sawdust was thrown on the road by the force of the impact. Cross-examined: I had a clear run. The other cars I had seen were right in front. When I got to Burwood road I put up my hand for him to ease, I did not pull up until after I was struck. When the car struck my cart it twisted all the axle up, split a spoke and broke the back end of a rail. He skidded my cart round. I got out after it occurred. If defendant said: "Are you hurt," I did not hear him. Defendant drove off after inspecting the front of his car. A lady offered the number of the car if I had not taken it myself. It has cost me 7/6 so far for repairs. Witness said he had seen defendant since the accident. Defendant asked him if he had come to pay for damages to the car. Witness replied in the negative, and said he wanted compensation for damages to his cart. If defendant had not struck him he would have brought the lamp down. To Mr. Henningsen: I was going up the road and he was coming down. Edward Wood, fruiterer, Auburn road, said he saw complainant coming up Auburn road and a motor car was coming down Burwood road. The "chap" on the cart seemed to spin round and the cart got a bad bump. The "chap" on the car asked the "chap" on the car to come back, but he drove away. Defendant was travelling fast — over 20 miles an hour. To Mr Philpott: The pace was dangerous to the public. To the inspector: I heard no horn sounded. Cross-examined: I was standing still. The pace was 20 to 24 miles an hour.

Defendant, on oath, certificated motor driver, Spring street, said he had never been in trouble before. The car was sent to his garage to be fixed up; it was a very old style of car. On the date in question he had been out to Box Hill. He wanted to test it with the hills. Coming down a hill he would be able to get about 15 miles an hour with the engine on. Complainant stopped in the centre of the road, as soon as ever witness wanted to get across the road complainant whipped up his horse to get across first. If he had been going at a rapid pace there would be none of the cart left. The paint was not even knocked off the car. Witness did all he could to avoid the collision, and had put on the brakes. If complainant had stopped where he had pulled up there would have been no collision. Cross-examined: I got to Box Hill by reversing when I got to some of the hills. I was going at about five miles an hour when I struck him. I defy anybody to get 24 miles out of the car. You won't get 15 miles out of it, I'll guarantee that. I swear that I did stop when I got to the bottom of the hill. The weight of the car — 25 cwt. — at four miles an hour would have turned the cart round. I hit him at ...

George Garlepp was charged with having taken from her mother and against the will of her father, with un-lawful intent, Grace Louisa Shore.

Mr. Corr, for accused, said this was a case of a young woman who fell in love with a young man. She went away herself and he afterwards assisted her. The girl was between 17 and 18 and had become a mother of a child. The mother and Grace were both willing that Grace should marry him. He thought marry and ....??...... He understood that the father was unwilling that a marriage should take place, but a magistrate could give consent.

Sub inspector Keegan said the case had gone too far. His instructions were to prosecute.

Mr Philpott: I really can't understand that you could have any better arrangement than that they should get married. We want to do the best we can in the circumstances. In my opinion the correct thing is to bring these young people together.

The sub Inspector: I don't think there is the slightest chance.

Mr Corr said he understood that the girl was willing to marry accused.

Grace Louisa Shore, domestic servant, said she had resided in Camberwell. She was now at the Salvation Army "Haven" at North Fitzroy. She had been "going with" accused for two years. Improper relations took place about three days after she first met accused. She met him about Christmas time, 1911. She remembered April, 1912. About 12 months ago she was living with her parents in Auburn road. She remembered meeting accused one morning at his home. They had a conversation and he asked her if she would marry him. She did not say anything.
He did not ask her to go away with him. she went herself. They went to Port Melbourne to one of accused's cousin's place and stopped there for the night. On the following morning they went to Williamstown to Johnston's house, near the beach station.
Accused told Mrs. Johnston that he would pay her board, that witness was his sister.
Mrs Johnston said she was not his sister. She remained there about six months.
Accused used to come there every Saturday night. Impropriety occurred from time to time.
Witness knew a Mrs MacDermott, and was employed by her as a domestic servant at No. 7 John Street. Accused visited her there every Saturday night for the three weeks she was there, also. Before leaving Mrs MacDermott's she asked accused if her mother wanted her at home and he said "No", that she did not want to have anything more to do with her.
She knew that she was then in a certain condition. After she told him of that he took her to Fitzroy to a place and left her there. She did not know the name of the place. She had a room to herself there. Accused stopped with her there for a night. He left her on a Monday morning and she did not see any more of him. She remained there for three weeks. She told the lady of the house of her condition and she took her to the Fitzroy police station.
Her father and mother told her not to go with accused.

Mr Corr objected. Accused was not present and it was not evidence.

To the sub inspector: When he asked me to marry him I said. "No".

To Mr Philpott: He did not ask me to go away with him. I went on my own.

Cross examined: The day before I left home my mother "roused" at me. She was so frightened that Constable Dunn had to take her to her own home on the following day. Accused and his sister took her to Constable Dunn because she would not go home. She was threatened to be beaten for speaking to "George". If she had her own will she would marry George. She used to go after George a great deal. She did not refuse to marry him that day when he asked her. The truth was that she said "Yes". She knew she could not get married without her parents' consent. She had asked accused to take her away with him the day before accused took her home. On the following day she cleared away from home. Accused did not know that she was going to clear away. She left home at about 7 a.m. and went to accused's place and knocked at his window. It was then about 8 o'clock. He did not know that she was coming. She ran away again because her father and mother were angry. She was "sweethearting" with somebody they did not want. He then told her she ought to go home, but she went to the kitchen and waited for him.

She got a cart and went to Caulfield. He did not know where she was. She got lost. Some fellow that was selling ferns picked her up there. At Caulfield she went to a lady's house and told her she had run away from home. It was not true that accused had induced her to run away from home. Accused found her afterwards. If accused's cousin said she had not stopped at Port Melbourne it was possible she had forgotten. Nearly all the time she was away she used to earn wages. The only time accused occupied a room with her was when he took her to Fitzroy. He said he was working at Lillydale and would be back at the end of the week. She had asked him to take her away, and he would not she ran away. All the time she was away he did not suggest to her to go home; she was not happy at home. She was still fond of him and would marry him now:-

To sub inspector Keegan: She was working at Williamstown. She had given birth to a child opposite "The Haven". North Fitzroy. It was a long time after she left Fitzroy before she saw him again.

Sydney George Shore, gardener said the former witness was his daughter. She was 17 last January. In April 1912, he was living in No. 7 Auburn Parade, Auburn. On April 1 he missed his daughter and went in search of her. He found her in Camberwell road with accused. Witness gave her two cuts with the cane and told her to go home. She went in the direction of home. Witness said that he told accused that his daughter was no fit girl to go about with and accused said he would have her in spite of him. When he found that she did not return he went to the police station and met Constable Dunn. They met accused and his sister and witness's daughter again. Witness lost his temper and threatened to hit accused over the head with a stick. Witness and Constable Dunn took his daughter home. She remained home until the following morning, but she got away between 7.30 and 8 on the following morning. Witness applied for her arrest on April 3 and did not see her for 12 months after at the Salvation Army "Haven" at North Fitzroy.

To Mr. Philpott: My daughter is deficient. Until 10 years of age she was not out of the ABC class. Dr Kent Hughes had examined her. During the whole time he had only given her 2/-.

Mr Corr: You are wrong.

Witness: I would not agree to him marrying her.

Cross examined: I have not been cruel to her. I struck her once with a cane in Camberwell Road. Witness's wife never ill-used the girl. The girl was infatuated with accused. and witness did his best to prevent it.

To Mr Philpott: The child was still born. The Salvation Army paid all the expenses.

Mr. Corr: He went to the house and offered to marry the girl but the mother threw him out.

Witness: The moment she was found he offered to marry her, but not until then.

To Mr Philpott: She got 12/6 a week at a factory. He would not consent to accused marrying her.

Annie Shore, married woman, said the girl was her daughter. She had a conversation with accused a week before Christmas. He came into her yard intoxicated and said he did not know where the girl was. He said he would marry the girl and witness said she would rather put through a mincing machine. On March 1 last, he came to witness and said he wanted to marry the girl as she was about to become a mother.

To Mr Philpott: I thought why did he not marry her before the time came so near.

To Mr Corr: I was agreeable to the marriage at first, but the father was against it. The girl was absolutely Infatuated with him. and the day before she ran away he helped to bring her home.

Mr Philpott: It is a long way from giving consent to marriage to the mincing machine. -

Constable Dunn said at about 11.30 p.m. on April 2 of last year he went from Shore to several houses ....?????.....Camberwell Road in the early hours of the morning. Accused said her father and mother had been very cruel to her. Her mother knocked her down in the right-of-way and dragged her up the lane by the hair of the head. The girl also said: "My father and mother are very cruel to me." Witness then ordered away and took the girl to her home.

To Mr Corr: Accused said they had been to the Camberwell police station, but could not make anybody hear there; and they were now going to look for a policeman. He had seen the girl in accused's company repeatedly. - Constable Rogers, stationed at Fitzroy said on April 10, 1912, he was stationed at Port Melbourne. He then had an interview with accused in Dow Street. He asked him what he had done with the girl, Grace Shore, and he said he did not where she was.

Donald MacDermott, chief petty officer of the Poonah of the Commonwealth naval forces, said the girl Shore was in his service from early in last May until February this year. Accused came to visit the girl at every weekend. He was there on the same night that she left. -

To Mr Corr: I was paying her 5/- a week all the time. -

Mary Maine, boarding house keeper, 146 Gore Street, Fitzroy said accused came to her under the name of Brown at the end of January or early in February and asked for a room for a married couple. He said he worked at Lilydale. The two occupied the room that night and he came on another occasion. The girl re-mained about one month with her, but witness did not see accused again. Subsequently witness took her to the police station in Fitzroy. Witness got 9/- or 10/- from accused. The girl was stranded and had nothing to eat and
witness kept her for some time for charity. -

To Mr Corr: She would not tell me where her mother lived. I don't think she had the fare to go home. He sent her 2/- but I suppose the unfortunate girl was afraid to go home. She had the opportunity to go home if she wished to. -

 Mr Corr argued that there was no evidence that accused took the girl away with intent. Accused took her home twice in one evening, instead of taking her away. She having gone away herself, there was no excuse for accused afterwards but still the subject of the charge had not been proved.

The Chairman: after brief retirement of the bench, said his own idea was that accused was a confirmed scamp, but there was not evidence to sustain a conviction.

The bench therefore had no option but to dismiss the case.

"THE HAVEN."

NEW MATERNITY HOME

DESCRIPTION OF THE PLACE.

The new Maternity Home of the Salvation Army, at North Fitzroy, will be opened by Lady Brassey to-morrow afternoon. The premises, as our readers have already been informed, are to be used for the helping of young women and girls who have got into trouble, and are friendless. Some description of the "Haven" will be read with interest in connection with the formal opening.

It is, first of all, to be remembered that Mrs Booth is to be congratulated on the excellent bargain she has made. The building, which is in Alfred Crescent, overlooking the Edinburgh Gardens, stands on three-quarters of an acre of land, and originally cost between five and six thousand pounds, to which may be added £1000 for the cost of the land. Mrs Booth has purchased it for 1,2000. The building is a two-storied one, with a broad verandah running all along the front. On one side is a garden laid out with shrubbery and choice flowers, which add a pleasing effect to the central entrance.

Passing through a door, we find ourselves in a spacious hall, and before us is a broad staircase, with massive polished banisters, above which is a magnificent stained glass window, the central figure of which is a lovely woman holding in her hand a harp. We pass into the room (16 x 14) at the left hand, which is suitably furnished as a reception room, and superintendent's office. Here, of course, visitors will be received. This room possesses a massive and costly marble mantelpiece, and is furnished with three bronze gas brackets, of up to-date design. A convenient door leads into the adjoining room, also large and airy, which is being set apart as the home workroom. Here the girls will do all manner of sewing, plain and fancy, useful and ornamental, babies' clothes, blouses, ladies' dresses, in fact, anything and everything that skilled fingers can make for those who wish to help them to support the institution and themselves.

We next enter the long and lofty dining room, with its shining beeswaxed floors. Beyond is a long dormitory, which was formerly used as a ballroom, but now is fitted with two rows of single bedsteads, with snowy sheeting and quilts, besides cots for the babies. Eighteen young women, exclusive of their offspring, can be accommodated here. A central aisle gives the dormitory quite a smart hospital ward appearance.

In the upper part of the premises, the front bedroom on the left is being set apart as a day nursery, where seven or eight cherubs may snooze or play, for, besides the comfortable cots, there are an equal number of baby chairs; and shortly, no doubt there will be a plentiful supply of nursery furniture in the shape of rocking horses, crowing ducks, "unbreakable" dolls, etc. Adjoining this is another dormitory, which will accommodate seven adults, and is very suitable indeed for the purpose to which it will be devoted. There are also substantial and useful wardrobes erected in convenient places.

Upstairs there is also another but much smaller dormitory than the one below, and which will contain some five beds. Near by is a back staircase which leads direct to the kitchen, scullery, and pantry. In the former, a huge range is being placed, in order that the cooking for such considerable numbers may be well and economically accomplished.

The home has been fitted by its former occupant with electric bells, and most useful they will be. Outside is an aviary and splendid stabling for two nags, with hayloft and stores above. There is a nice lawn adjoining the Home, and also a kitchen garden and drying grounds. The whole of the buildings are substantially built, and are connected externally. All the fittings are of a most modern and

I suggested earlier that I would like to share some information about "The Haven" where Grace found herself, as she was pregnant and had, in her mind, had no other choices.

It was common practice, for unmarried, young pregnant women to live in places like this until the birth of the baby.

The article on the right is a fantastic description of "The Haven". This article was found in

The Herald on Herald on14 May 1897,

I have transcribed the article on the following page.

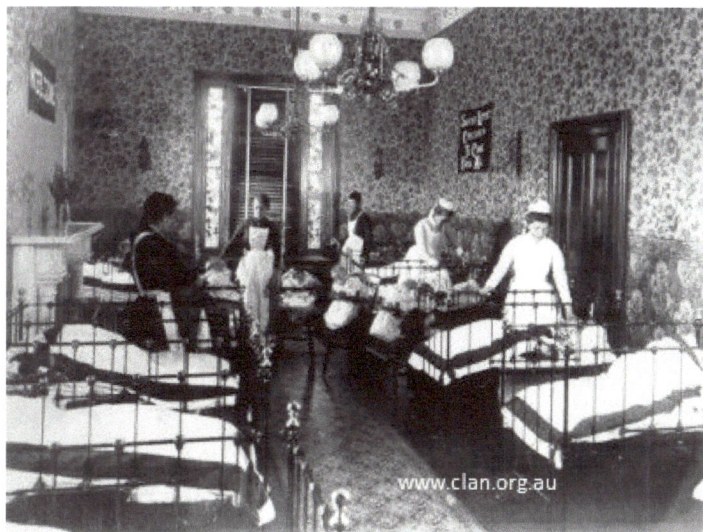

www.clan.org.au

"THE HAVEN."NEW MATERNITY HOME DESCRIPTION OF THE PLACE.

The new Maternity Home of the Salvation Army, at North Fitzroy, will be opened by Landy Brassey tomorrow afternoon. The premises, as our readers have already been informed, are to be used for the helping of young women and girls who have got into trouble, and are friendless.

Some description of the "Haven" will be read with interest in connection with the formal opening. It is, first of all, to be remembered that Mrs Booth is to be congratulated on the excellent bargain she has made. The building, which is in Alfred Crescent, overlooking the Edinburgh Gardens stands on three quarters of an acre of land and originally cost between five and six thousand pounds, to which may be added L1000 for the cost of the land. Mrs Booth has purchased it for L2000.

The building is a two storied one, with a broad verandah running all along the front. On one side is a garden tastily laid out with shrubbery and choice flowers, which add a pleasing effect to the central entrance. Passing through a door, we find ourselves in a spacious hall, and before us is a broad staircase, with massive polished bannisters, above which is a magnificent stained glass window, the central figure of which is a lovely woman, holding in her hand a harp. We pass into the room (15x14) at the left hand, which is suitably furnished as a reception room, and superintendent's office. Here, of course, visitors will be received. This room possesses a massive and costly marble mantelpiece, and is furnished with three bronze gas brackets of up to date design.

A convenient door leads into the adjoining room, also large and airy, which is being set apart as the home workroom. Here the girls will do all manner of sewing, plain and fancy, useful and ornamental, babies clothes, blouses, ladies dresses, in fact anything and everything that skilled fingers can make for those who wish to help them to support the institution and themselves.

We next enter the long and lofty dining room with its shining beeswaxed floors. Beyond is a long dormitory, which was formerly used as a ballroom, but now is fitted with two rows of single bedsteads, with snowy sheeting and quilts, besides cots for the babies. Eighteen young women, exclusive of their offspring, can be accommodated here. A central aisle gives the dormitory quite a smart hospital ward appearance. In the upper part of the premises, the front bedroom on the left is being set apart as a day nursery, where seven or eight cherubs may snooze or play, for, besides the comfortable cots, there are an equal number of baby chairs; and shortly, no doubt there will be a plentiful supply of nursery furniture in the shape of rocking horses, crowing cocks, "unbreakable" dolls, etc.

Adjoining this is another dormitory, which will accommodate seven adults, and is very suitable indeed for the purpose to which it will be devoted. There are also substantial and useful wardrobes erected in convenient places. Upstairs there is also another but much smaller dormitory than the one below, and which will contain some five beds.

Near by is a back stair case, which leads direct to the kitchen, scullery, and pantry. In the former, a huge range is being placed, in order that the cooking for such considerable numbers may be well and economically accomplished.

The home has been fitted by its former occupant with electric bells, and most useful they will be. Outside is an aviary and splendid stabling for two nags, with hayloft and stores above. There is a nice lawn adjoining the Home, and also a kitchen garden and drying grounds. The whole of the buildings are substantially built and are cemented externally. All the fittings are of a most modern and tasteful character.

In 1914, George Patrick and Grace Louisa Shore were married. Grace was born, Victoria in 1895, to Sidney George Shore (1859–1918) and Catherine Ann (Annie Jane) Shore (nee Shepherd 1872–1914)

Grace was the 3rd child of 10. Grace's mother died Cerebral Thrombosis, 6 months after giving birth to her last child from . This was in 1914, not long after the fiasco with Grace and George.

George and Grace had the following children:

William Roy Garlepp	1915–1998
Edward Patrick Garlepp	1917–1974
George Patrick Garlepp	1918–1978
Kathleen Mary Garlepp	1920–1980
Agnes "Pat" Garlepp	1925–2000
John Patrick Garlepp	1928–1955

This is the first time I've come across a family that gave the same middle name to most of their sons and one of their daughters took on the nick name Pat. William Roy as the odd man out. He was named after Grace's brother who died when he was a toddler in 1907.

George and Grace were living at 183 Camberwell Road, Upper Hawthorn, Victoria when George enlisted in the army on 29 October, 2017.

On the next few pages I will share his military records. You will see that he gave his birth as 8 May, 1893 rather than 1891. His birth was registered as 1891. Was he more attractive to the military if he was two years younger?

We also find that he was working as a Driver at the time.

George applied twice, firstly on 4 February, 1916 and then 29 October, 1917. Either he wasn't accepted the first time, or he changed his mind.

George was sent to France and in December, 1918 Absented himself without leave for a few months. He surrendered and was given 2 years jail sentence and was sent to Dunkirk. He was released 21 July 1919, with his sentence suspended. He returned home 7 September, 1919. He was discharged 2 March, 2020.

A206350

now 1000   38 Bn

AUSTRALIAN ✠ MILITARY FORCES.

AUSTRALIAN IMPERIAL FORCE.

Attestation Paper of Persons Enlisted for Service Abroad.

No. 3304

Name in full { Surname **GARLEPP** / Christian Name *George*

V 70393

Unit   8/38 RFTS.

Joined on   OCT 29 1917

Questions to be put to the Person Enlisting before Attestation.

You are hereby warned that if after enlistment it is found that you have given a wilfully false answer to any question set forth in this Attestation Paper, you will be liable to be tried for the offence.

1. What is your Name?	1. *George Garlepp*
2. In or near what Town were you born?	2. In or near the Town of *Port Melbourne* In the State or Country of *Victoria*
3. Are you a natural born British Subject or a Naturalized British Subject? (N.B.—If the latter, papers to be shown.)	3. *Natural Born British Subject*
4. What is your Age? (Date of birth to be stated)	4. *24 5/12 years* *8th May 1893*
5. What is your Trade or Calling?	5. *Driver*
6. Are you, or have you been, an Apprentice? If so, where, to whom, and for what period?	6. *No*
7. Are you married, single, or widower?	7. *Married*
8. Who is your next of kin? (Address and relationship to be stated) The answer to this question shall not be construed as in the nature of a Will.	8. *Wife — Grace Garlepp, 183 Camberwell Road Upper Hawthorn Victoria*
9. What is your permanent address in Australia?	9. *183 Camberwell Road Upper Hawthorn Victoria.*
10. Do you now belong to, or have you ever served in, His Majesty's Army, the Marines, the Militia, the Militia Reserve, the Territorial Force, Royal Navy, or Colonial Forces? If so, state which, and if not now serving, state cause of discharge	10. *No*
11. Have you stated the whole, if any, of your previous service?	11. —
12. Have you ever been rejected as unfit for His Majesty's Service? If so, on what grounds?	12. *No*
13. (For married men, widowers with children, and soldiers who are the sole support of widowed mother)— Do you understand that no separation allowance will be issued in respect of your service beyond an amount which together with pay would reach ten shillings per day?	13. *Yes*
14. Are you prepared to undergo inoculation against small pox and enteric fever?	14. *Yes*

I, *George Garlepp* do solemnly declare that the above answers made by me to the above questions are true, and I am willing and hereby voluntarily agree to serve in the Military Forces of the Commonwealth of Australia within or beyond the limits of the Commonwealth.

And I further agree to allot not less than ~~two-fifths~~ three-fifths of the pay payable to me from time to time during my service for the support of my ~~wife.†~~ wife and children.

Date *5th Oct. 1917.*

George Garlepp

Signature of Person Enlisted.

* This clause should be struck out in the case of unmarried men or widowers without children under 16 years of age.
† Two-fifths must be allotted to the wife, and if there are children three-fifths must be allotted.

D.349/4.17.—C.7814.—50m.

2

CERTIFICATE OF ATTESTING OFFICER.

The foregoing questions were read to the person enlisted in my presence.

I have taken care that he understands each question, and that his answer to each question has been duly entered as replied to by him.

I have examined his naturalization papers and am of opinion that they are correct.

(This to be struck out except in the case of persons who are naturalized British Subjects.)

Date 5th Oct. 1917

C. N. Brown Parker J.P.

Signature of Attesting Officer.

OATH TO BE TAKEN BY PERSON BEING ENLISTED.*

3, George Garlepp _____ swear that I will well and truly serve our Sovereign Lord the King in the Australian Imperial Force from 5th October 1917 until the end of the War, and a further period of four months thereafter unless sooner lawfully discharged, dismissed, or removed therefrom; and that I will resist His Majesty's enemies and cause His Majesty's peace to be kept and maintained; and that I will in all matters appertaining to my service, faithfully discharge my duty according to law.

So Help Me, God.

George Garlepp

Signature of Person Enlisted.

Taken and subscribed at Hawthorn in the State of Victoria this 5th day of October 1917, before me—

C. N. Brown Parker, J.P.

Signature of Attesting Officer.

*A person enlisting who objects to taking an oath may make an affirmation in accordance with the Third Schedule of the Act, and the above form must be amended accordingly. All amendments must be initialed by the Attesting Officer.

Description of *George Garlepp* [3] on Enlistment.

Age _24_ years _5_ months.

Height _5_ feet _7½_ inches.

Weight _15-8_ lbs.

Chest Measurement _31½ – 34_ inches.

Complexion _fair_

Eyes _grey_

Hair _fair_

Religious Denomination _R. C._

DISTINCTIVE MARKS.

3 Vac. left
Tattoos both forearms viz

L arm Horse Shoe woman head
Horses head
R. arm Thistle B. O
Heart and crown

CERTIFICATE OF MEDICAL EXAMINATION.

I HAVE examined the above-named person, and find that he does not present any of the following conditions, viz. :—

Scrofula; phthisis; syphilis; impaired constitution; defective intelligence; defects of vision, voice, or hearing; hernia; hæmorrhoids; varicose veins, beyond a limited extent; marked varicocele with unusually pendent testicle; inveterate cutaneous disease; chronic ulcers; traces of corporal punishment; contracted or deformed chest; abnormal curvature of spine; or any other disease or physical defect calculated to unfit him for the duties of a soldier.

He can see the required distance with either eye; his heart and lungs are healthy; he has the free use of his joints and limbs; and he declares he is not subject to fits of any description.

I consider him fit for active service.

Date _5/10/17_

Place _Hawthorn_

_____
Signature of Examining Medical Officer.

CERTIFICATE OF COMMANDING OFFICER.

I CERTIFY that this Attestation of the above-named person is correct, and that the required forms have been complied with. I accordingly approve, and appoint him

to _8/38 RFTS._

Date _DEC 10 1917_

Place _BROADMEADOWS_

_____ LIEUT.
O.C. 8/38

Commanding _8/38 RFTS._

Statement of Service of No. **3301** Name *GARLEPP. George.*

Unit in which served.	Promotions, Reductions, Casualties, &c.	Period of service in each rank.		Remarks.
		From—	To—	
RECRUIT DEPOT Broadmeadows	Private	OCT 13 1917	29/10/17	Infantry.
2nd Batt B'meadows 8/38 h Rfts	"	29/10/17	22/12/17	
8/38 RFTS.	Private	DEC 22 1917		H M T. A38 Embarked
	Disembarked Southampton 14.2.18			L 1349 18·2·18
	Pte. M/S to 10th Trg Bn. Sutta Mandeville from Australia.	Jry	14·2·18	D/o 18/65 E 4-3-18 L 1439.
	Pte. offence Covant 20.4.18 a. m. 2 from 2200 to 20.4.18 until 2300 on 21. 4. 18. award 7 days C.B. by Major J. M. Hawkey. Forfeit 2 days pay R.W.		22. 4. 18	D/o 36/11782. 9.5.18 B2069 L 3724
	Pte. offence Covant 27.4.18 a d-dson 8·15 a m parade on 27. 4. 8. award 4 days F.p. No 2 by Major C.J. Keily		27. 4. 18	D/o 36/117 4 E. 9. 5. 18. L 3724 B2069
ex 10th Trg. Bn:	Pte. Proceeding Overseas FRANCE Covant via Folkestone	13·5·18		D/o 38/1307 E. L 3973 16-5-18
	Pte. offence Covant 9.5.18. Without urgent necessity quitting the ranks. award 7 days. F.P. No 2 by Major H. Jardine Blake. PO. No 66 y 55 4/16	Jry	10·5·18.	B E F D/o24 /2209 27. 5·18 L4164 12-6-18
	Pte. M/S to a.9.B.D from U.K. ex Reinft. 8/39th	France	14·5·18	D/o 23/2060. 5·6·18.
Pte	Pte. T.OS of 38th Batt. a.9.7 from 8th Reinfo	"	17. 5. 18.	D/o 23/2110. 5·6·18.

I have examined the above details, and find them correct in every respect.

———————————————————

STATEMENT OF SERVICE OF N.º 3304   NAME Garlepp George

Unit.	Promotions, Reductions, Casualties, etc.	Place.	Date.	Remarks.
	The Court of Enquiry held in the Field on the 15ᵗʰ October 1918 declared that N.º 3304 Pte Garlepp. G. illegally absented himself without leave from 38ᵗʰ Btn. A.I.F. on 13ᵗʰ Sept 1918 & that he is still so absent.	France		D/o 44/5485. 30.10.18
	38ᵗʰ Bn.			DO 120/689 11/11/18
Pte	" "			DO 4/1293/19
	Pte. 38 Bn			DO 15/515/19
	" "			D/o 48/363. 1919
				Do 128/147/19
				Do 144/180/19
				Do 160/74/19
Pte	RETURN TO AUSTRALIA Per Euripides	Eng.	6/9/19	X mR. 201. 1B R. 801 A 206250.

Page 1 (B).

STATEMENT OF SERVICE OF No. 3304 NAME GARLEPP

Unit.	Promotions, Reductions Casualties, etc.	Place.	Date.	Remarks.

Embarked 22/12/17

I ha... Discharged 3MD TPE 1/3/20

NAA: B2455, GARLEPP G.

A.I.F. 3304. Army Form B103 Part I.	Regtl. No.
	PRESENT UNIT 38th Battalion.
Service and Casualty Form.	3304.
PART I.	
380 s — 4/18 — 12344.	Present Rank Pte.	SURNAME GARLEPP
	Decorations	Christian Names. George.

Particulars.

Date of Enlistment	5.10.17.	Place of Enlistment	Hawthorn.Vic:
Age on Enlistment	24 Years 5 Months	Any subsequent claim as to age after verification of Birth Certificate Auth. C.R.	Years Months / /
Birthplace	Melbourne. Vic:	Religion	R.C.
		If Married	Yes.
Trade or Calling	Driver	If an Apprentice	No.
Date of Embarkation from Australia	22/12/14.	Whereabouts of Next of Kin, i.e. Australia or Abroad	AUST
		Special Notification Card No.	

NAA: B2455, GARLEPP G.

Nothing to be written in this Margin.

CASUALTY FORM—ACTIVE SERVICE.

Army Form B. 103.

Regiment or Corps .... Rank *Private* Name *Garlepp George*

Regimental No. *3304*

Enlisted (a) *13/10/17*. Terms of Service (a) *Duration of War* Service reckons from (a) *13/10/17*.

Date of appointment to lance rank }

Numerical position on roll of N.C.O.'s }

Extended .... Re-engaged .... Qualification (b) ....

Date.	Report. From whom Received.	Record of promotions, reductions, transfers, casualties, &c., during active service, as reported on Army Form B. 213, Army Form A. 36, or in other official documents. The authority to be quoted in each case.	Place.	Date.	Remarks taken from Army Form B. 213, Army Form A. 36, or other official documents.
1 22/12/17	O.C.Troops	Emb̄ 6y Syd 38ᵗʰ Illawarra	Melbourne	22/2/17	
2 16/1/18	C.O.Troops	Disembarked to A.I.F. Camp	Suez	16/1/18.	
3 24/1/18	C.O.Troops	Embarked H.M.T. Leasowe Castle	Port Said	24/1/18.	
4 2/3/18	O.C.Troops	Disembarked	Taranto	2/3/18	✓ 1549. 18/2/18
			Southampton	14.2.18	S 14/39 43.2.17
5 14.2.18	O.C. 10ᵗʰ Bng Bn	(P.O.) Proc. from Aust.	Eng	14.2.18	S Q.18/1653 B.14.2.18
6 17.3.18	O.C. Ly Bn	Inflicted S.W. oᵇᵃʸ R.O.719 of 22.6.14 in field to wd wd at Ashbury at 11. a.m. 14.3.18 Inflicted S.W. by Award & hay. G.B. by Major G.S.J. Kerby	Perham Sutton Mandeville 14.3.18	16.3.18.	B 20.69. L 2541

(c) In the case of a man who has re-engaged for, or enlisted into section D. Army Reserve, particulars of such re-engagement or enlistment will be entered.

(b) e.g., Signaller, Shoeing Smith, &c., &c., also special qualifications in technical Corps duties. (P.T.O.)

D.002/A.16—C.7316—8181

Report.		Record of promotions, reductions, transfers, casualties, &c., during active service, as reported on Army Form B. 213, Army Form A. 36, or in other official documents. The authority to be quoted in each case.	Place.	Date.	Remarks taken from Army Form B. 213, Army Form A. 36, or other official documents.
Date.	From whom Received.				
28.4.18	G.O.R.O. Inf. By Ba.	Pte. A. to L. Returned	Lovant	20.4.18.	P.2 2097.
27.4.18	O.C. G.D. Inf. Ba.	Pte. Offence Lovant 20.4.18. A.9r. of fur 2200.07 20.4.18. In al 2300 or 21.4.10 Award 4 days F.P. by Major L.Dn. Hawkey 22.4.18 Forfeits 2 days pay Pte.		21.4.18.	86.36/ E. 9.5.18 L.3424 B2069.
27.4.18	" "	Pte. Offence Lovant 27.4.16 A.9r.L. from 8.15.a.m. Parade or 27.4.18. Award Adys F.P. No.2 by Major C.J. Reily 27.4.18		22.4.18.	86.36/ E 9.5.18 L.3424 B2069
12.5.18	9 Aus Inf Bn	Pte. Proceeding Overseas FRANCE ex Lovant via Folkestone		27.4.18. 10.5.18 13.5.18	86.38/ E. 16.5. L.3973.
14.5.18	NZ B/Der Pte	Marched in Ex. Eng.	Etaples	14.5.18	Alcsay.D.O 23/
15.18	" "	Marched out to Front		16.5.18	Alcsay/57 D.O 23/XII6
25.5.18	B 213.38 d. Bn 9 Aug Bn	Taken on Strength	Field	17.5.18	cAufg 4.18y/8 AlB49/8 D.O 24/5/09
		Offence without urgent necessity Servant 9.5.18 Award 14 days F.P.N 2 by Major Farant 10.5.18		10.5.18	
13.7.18	APM 39 w Bn.	Reported on Absence		4.7.18	
14.8.18	Do	Arrested at Fobin Bochum			
9.11	Do	Reported on Absence			

Army Form B. 103—II.
Part II.

Shody

(SERVICE AND CASUALTY FORM Part II).

Regiment or Corps _38Bn_   Surname _Garlepp_   Christian Names _George_   Regimental Number _3304_

*Substantive Rank _Pte_

*Acting Rank _____
(* To be entered in pencil to facilitate alteration.)

(A) Report		(B) Authority of Part II. of Orders	(C) Record of promotions, appointments, reductions, casualties, transfers, postings, &c., All acting as well as substantive promotions to be shown, for method of entry of which see A.C.I, 1816 of 1917. Corps and unit to which transferred and posted to be invariably named.	(D) Place of casualty	(E) Date of promotion, reduction, reversion, casualty, &c.	(F) Remarks, and initials and rank of an officer
Date	From whom received					
15.10.15	CO 38Bn	20/44/SMES	De Declared on George Absented	head	13.9.18	1/31c/13/3
14.9.18	"		Offence WOAS AWL from 9 pm 3.7.18 Kinde apprehended by MP at 11.40 am 18.7.18 Award 28 days FPNº2 by CO 38Bn			C114/93-101 20.14/63/94/05
			Total Forf 14 days Pay	head	12.9.18	
			" Rejoined unit ex Illegal Absen "		7.12.18	404/293 C114/108
14.12.18	"	Party	99th head 19.12.18			
Jan 18	"		Charge Morning himself w/b Reserve w/had ke at Henr Mellaire at 22.30 on 13/9/18 absented himself & remand attack into surrendering himself to him Lath Nº2 at SAPEL at 15.30 on 1/12/18 Surg: Sentence 2 years 1.HL.19 12.18. Confirmed by CO 10-A1B 17. n.18 Promulgated 21/12/18. Commenced /ration 8/12/18			C/114/109 DO 15/515
			Pte Adm.			
8.2.19	Nº1 MP			Lords Mague/2 2.19 Mo20 20.49/363 1919.

Nothing to be written in this margin.

(A) Report Date.	From whom received	(B) Authority of Part II. of Orders	(C) Record of promotions, appointments, reductions, casualties, transfers, postings, &c.; as subsequent promotion to substantive rank, active or out of entry of which see A.C.I. 1810 of 1917. Corps and unit to which transferred and posted to be invariably named.	(D) Place of casualty	(E) Date of promotion, reduction, reversion, casualty, &c.	(F) Remarks, and initials and rank of an officer
28.6.19	10 M.P.	Re. Trans to UK		Dunkirk 22.6.19		M6244
23.6.19	NR.E.S.O	" Dysenb x 10 Mil Prison Agnes (under escort)		Folkstone		LX6071
		Evac. to Wandsworth Prison (Auth HQ BT in F and F wire No.1.S 221 § 11.6.19)			22.6.19	Do 128/147
		Ref. Do 15/515/19 Do 48/363/19 Sentence augh.				Do 144/180
23.7.18	HQ AIF Depôt in UK	21.7.19 on release from Prison (PRAIF-B280/146/61)		Sidworth 21.7.19		L9 6810
4.8.19	Depôt Camp	" MP. to Depôt Camp			cc 6573	
		Offence: Forward 2.8.19		Forward 2.8.19		
		NM.L. 2359 2.8.19 Ad 1500 2.8.19		1500 2.8.19		co 160/94 14.8.19
		Award. Admonished by				14.8.19
		Colyer. A M? Kinnon.			4.8.19	
		Total forfeiture 1 day's pay.				
		RETURN TO AUSTRALIA Per Euripides			Eng 1919 Melbourne	
		Decembarked				

CONFIDENTIAL

AR.

16th February.   21

Deputy Commissioner,
  Department of Repatriation,
    Victorian Branch,
      St. Kilda Road,
        MELBOURNE.

                    In response to your request per telephone of the
15th February.,furnished hereunder are the particulars you desire in
connection with ex No. 3304 Private George GARLEPP, 38th Battalion:-.

 5/10/17. Enlisted in the A.I.F.
22/12/17. Embarked for Active Service Abroad.
16/1/18. Disembarked at Suez, and proceeded to A.I.F. Camp.
24/1/18. Embarked at Port Said.
 2/2/18. Disembarked at Taranto.
14/2/18. Disembarked at Southampton, England.
14/2/18. Marched into 10th Training Battalion, England, ex
         Australia.
16/3/18. Awarded 3 days' C.B. for neglect to obey order, for
         being without a pass 11 a.m. 14/3/18.
20/4/18. Reported A.W.L.
21/4/18. Returned ex A.W.L.
22/4/18. Awarded 7 days' C.B. for being A.W.L. 20/4/18 till
         21/4/18.,forfeits 2 days' pay under R.W.
27/4/18. Awarded 4 days' F.P.No.2 for being A.W.L. from 8.15
         a.m. parade on 27/4/18.
10/5/18. Awarded 7 days' F.P.No.2 for without urgent necessity
         quitting the ranks, 9/5/18.
13/5/18. Proceeded Overseas to France, ex England.
14/5/18. Marched into New Zealand Base Depot, Etaples, ex
         England.
16/5/18. Marched out to Front.
17/5/18. Taken on strength 38th Battalion.
 4/7/18. Reported an Absentee.
x 18/8/18. Arrested at Vieliers Bocage.
13/9/18. Declared an Illegal Absentee.
 7/12/18. Rejoined Unit, ex Illegal Absentee.
x12/9/18. Awarded 28 days' F.P.No.2 for being A.W.L. 3/7/18
         until apprehended by M.P. 18/8/18.
19/12/18. F.G.C.M. CHARGE . Absenting himself without leave on
         13/9/18,and remained absent until surrendering
         himself on 7/12/18. SENTENCE. 2 years I.H.L.
 2/2/19. Admitted to No.7 Military Prison, Les Attagues.
22/6/19. Transferred to England.
22/6/19. Disembarked at Folkestone, ex No.10 Military Prison,
         France, under escort, and proceeded to Wandsworth
         Prison.
21/7/19. Marched into Details Camp,from A.I.F.Depots in U.K.
21/7/19. Sentence suspended on release from Prison.
 4/8/19. Admonished for being A.W.L. 2/8/19 till 3/8/19.
 3/9/19. Left England for return to Australia perH.T.
         "Euripides".
20/10/19. Disembarked Melbourne. --Demobilization.
 2/3/20. Discharged from the Australian Imperial Force,--
         termination of period of enlistment.

Major
Officer 1/c Base Records.

In 1924, George and Grace were living at 209 Camberwell Road, Auburn and George had returned to being a Driver.

Grace died on 7 October, 1953 at home at 361 Riversdale Road, Hawthorn. She was buried at Burwood cemetery. George died 27 February at the age of and was buried with Grace. Their son, John Patrick died in 1954 and is buried with them.

One more interesting piece of news about George and Grace, is that George's sister, Mary Agnes, and Grace's brother Sidney married in 1926.

Edward Garlepp was the youngest child of Henry and Catherine Garlepp. He was born in 1901 in Hawthorn, Victoria.

Edward married Sophia Agnes Smith (1902-1968). Sophia was the daughter of Ernest Edward Smith (1881–1967) and Wilhelmina Frances Smith (nee Watson 1878–1918)

Edward and Sophia had a daughter, Nancy who was born around 1930. On 23 November, 1931 Edward died. According to the notices put into the Age there was some confusion about his death. Some calling it an accident and then being changed.

129

In 1932, Edwards wife Sophia was in court for harbouring criminals. An article was found in the Age 1 September, 1932. The picture is on the following page, and below I have transcribed it.

Age (Melbourne, Vic. : 1854 - 1954), Thursday 1 September 1932, page 3

HARBOR FOR CRIMINALS.

WIDOW'S "OPEN HOUSE" POLICE RAID AT HAWTHORN !

Evidence that a young woman, whose only means of subsistence was a sustenance allowance of 6/ and an allowance of 8/ from the Children's Welfare department, had kept "open house" for men dis charged from Pentridge was given at Hawthorn court yesterday, when Sophia Agnes Garlepp, 27 years, widow, was charged with being the occupier of a house frequented by known and reputed thieves, or persons having insufficient lawful means of support.

Doreen Alice King, 30 years, married; Ernest William Andrews, 40 years salesman; Norman Richard Stevens, 27 years laborer; and Raymond Stevens, 25 years, laborer, were each charged with having been found in a house so frequented.

Plain clothes Constable Gooden said about 8.30 a.m. on 25th August, with other police, he went to a house in Station Street, Auburn, where he saw the five accused. He said to King, "We have had this place under observation, and we find it full of thieves. What is your excuse for being here?" She replied, "I am here with Mr. Andrews. He is keeping me." Witness said, "He cannot keep himself, He came out of gaol two months ago, and he has robbed people in almost every country in the world." King replied, "he gets remittances." Andrews was dressed in a pair of very short trousers and a woman's coat. He said he had pawned his clothes.

Raymond and Norman Stevens admitted they had no money, and had done no work since they were discharged from gaol at the beginning of August.

Garlepp admitted she was the occupier of the house. Asked her reason for having reputed thieves there she replied. "I would not turn them out. They come here from Pentridge, and I let them stay." She admitted her only means of support was 6/ sustenance allowance and 8/ from the Children's Welfare department in respect of her child. Witness asked where Raymond Stevens slept, and was told "in the ba-by's cot."

Garlepp admitted she knew that Norman Stevens had recently been discharged from gaol after serving eighteen months' imprisonment, and that Andrew's had recently completed a sentence of eighteen months in Tasmania for false pretences. She said she had met a man named Asling at the Melbourne Hospital and had sent various men discharged from gaol to her home. She admitted she knew convicted thieves named Jockey Jack, Hillard and Burriss.

Andrews was known to witness as an international criminal, with convictions in England, America, Canada and several Australian States. The two Stevens were convicted persons, and they, King and Garlepp were associates of known and reputed thieves.

Documentary evidence was submitted by R. C. Barnett that Andrews received monthly remittances from England of £21, plus exchange.

Andrews, on oath, said he and King lived together as man and wife. They returned from Hobart early in August, and on grounds of economy had accepted Mrs Garlepp's offer to stay at her home, Garlepp was King's sister.

Norman Stevens said he was formerly a licenced jockey. On release from prison he had 2 pounds 13 and his brother about five pounds. They had stayed at East Melbourne for a fortnight. He had then met Mrs Garlepp and agreed to rent a room from her. He and his brother had rationed themselves since.

Garlepp said she had known Norman Stevens three years previously.

She had suggested to her sister that she and Andrews should stay at her home, as she knew they had little money until Andrews received his next remittance.

Sentences of imprisonment for three months were imposed on Norman and Raymond Stevens. Garlepp was similarly sentenced, the sentence being suspended upon her entering into a bond of £20 to be of good behavior for twelve months. The charges against Andrews and King were dismissed.

A Family Heirloom. Garlepp was further charged with being found in possession of an unregistered pistol. Plain clothes Constable Gooden said that when searching a wardrobe he found the weapon, which, although small, would fire .22 calibre bullets. Mr Barnett said the weapon had belonged to Garlepp's father in law and had been used by her child as a toy. A fine of £1 was imposed, and an order for the confiscation of the weapon was made. made.

HARBOR FOR CRIMINALS.

WIDOW'S "OPEN HOUSE"

POLICE RAID AT HAW-THORN.

Evidence that a young woman, whose only means of subsistence was a sustenance allowance of 6/ and an allowance of 8/ from the Children's Welfare department, had kept "open house" for men discharged from Pentridge was given at Hawthorn court yesterday, when Sophia Agnes Garlepp, 27 years, widow, was charged with being the occupier of a house frequented by known and reputed thieves, or persons having insufficient lawful means of support. Doreen Alice King, 30 years, married; Ernest William Andrews, 40 years, salesman; Norman Richard Stevens, 27 years, laborer; and Raymond Stevens, 25 years, laborer, were each charged with having been found in a house so frequented.

Plain-clothes Constable Gooden said about 8.30 a.m. on 25th August, with other police, he went to a house in Station-street, Auburn, where he saw the five accused. He said to King, "We have had this place under observation, and we find it full of thieves. What is your excuse for being here?" She replied, "I am here with Mr. Andrews. He is keeping me." Witness said, "He cannot keep himself. He came out of gaol two months ago, and he has robbed people in almost every country in the world." King replied, "He gets remittances." Andrews was dressed in a pair of very short trousers and a woman's coat. He said he had pawned his clothes. Raymond and Norman Stevens admitted they had no money, and had done no work since they were discharged from gaol at the beginning of August. Garlepp admitted she was the occupier of the house. Asked her reason for having reputed thieves there she replied, "I would not turn them out. They come here from Pentridge, and I let them stay." She admitted her only means of support was 6/ sustenance allowance and 8/ from the Children's Welfare department in respect of her child. Witness asked where Raymond Stevens slept, and was told "in the baby's cot." Garlepp admitted she knew that Norman Stevens had recently been discharged from gaol after serving eighteen months' imprisonment, and that Andrews had recently completed a sentence of eighteen months in Tasmania for false pretences. She said she had met a man named Asling at the Melbourne Hospital, and he had sent various men discharged from gaol to her home. She admitted she knew convicted thieves named Jockey Jack, Hillard and Burriss. Andrews was known to witness as an international criminal, with convictions in England, America, Canada and several Australian States. The two Stevens were convicted persons, and they, King and Garlepp were associates of known and reputed thieves.

Documentary evidence was submitted to Mr. C. Barnett that Andrews received monthly remittances from England of £21, plus exchange.

Andrews, on oath, said he and King lived together as man and wife. They returned from Hobart early in August, and on grounds of economy had accepted Mrs. Garlepp's offer to stay at her home. Garlepp was King's sister.

Norman Stevens said he was formerly a licensed jockey. On release from prison he had £2 13/, and his brother about £5. They had stayed at East Melbourne for a fortnight. He had then met Mrs. Garlepp, and agreed to rent a room from her. He and his brother had rationed themselves since.

Garlepp said she had known Norman Stevens three years previously. She had suggested to her sister that she and Andrews should stay at her home, as she knew they had little money until Andrews received his next remittance.

Sentences of imprisonment for three months were imposed on Norman and Raymond Stevens. Garlepp was similarly sentenced, the sentence being suspended upon her entering into a bond of £20 to be of good behaviour for twelve months. The charges against Andrews and King were dismissed.

A Family Heirloom.

Garlepp was further charged with being found in possession of an unregistered pistol.

Plain-clothes Constable Gooden said that when searching a wardrobe he found the weapon, which, although small, would fire .22 calibre bullets.

Mr Barnett said the weapon had belonged to Garlepp's father-in-law, and had been used by her child as a toy.

A fine of £1 was imposed, and an order for the confiscation of the weapon was made.

SOCIAL SERVICES ABUSED.

Prosecutions at Hawthorn.

The receipt of sustenance money and of an allowance from the Children's Welfare department was admitted by Sophia Agnes Patricia Garlepp, aged 27 years, Station street, Auburn, who was charged at the Hawthorn Court yesterday with between August 4 and 25 having been the occupier of a house frequented by known and reputed thieves and persons having insufficient lawful means of support. Ernest William Andrews, aged 40 years, salesman, Norman Robert Stevens, aged 27 years, and Raymond Stevens, aged 27 years, his brother, were each charged with having been found in a house frequented by known and reputed thieves or persons having insufficient lawful means of support.

Plain clothes Constable Gooden said that he and other constables found Andrews sleeping on a sofa, and Raymond Stevens sleeping in a child's cot. In a wardrobe they found a pistol. Garlepp said, "I would not turn them out. They came here from Pentridge and I let them stay." She admitted that she received sustenance at the rate of 6/ a week, and also received 8/ a week from the Children's Welfare department for her child.

For the defence of Andrews bank correspondence was produced showing that he was in receipt of a remittance from England. He was discharged.

Garlepp was convicted and sentenced to imprisonment for three months, but an order was made suspending the sentence upon Garlepp entering into a bond of £20 to be of good behaviour for a year. She was also convicted on a charge of having been in possession of an unregistered pistol and was fined £1. An order was made for the confiscation of the weapon.

Norman Stevens and Raymond Stevens, who both admitted previous convictions, were each sentenced to imprisonment for three months.

Here is another article found in the Argus on1 September 1932. I have transcribed it below.

SOCIAL SERVICES ABUSED.
Prosecutions at Hawthorn.

The receipt of sustenance money and of an allowance from the Children's welfare department was admitted by Sophia Agnes Patricia Garlepp, aged 27 years, Station street, Auburn, who was charged at the Hawthorn Court yesterday with between August 4 and 25 having being the occupier of a house frequented by known and reputed thieves and persons having insufficient lawful means of support. Ernest William Andrews, aged 40 years, salesman; Norman Robert Stevens aged 27 years; and Raymond Stevens, aged 27 years, his brother, were each charged with having been found in a house frequented by known and reputed thieves or persons having insufficient lawful means of support.

Plain clothes Constable Gooden said that he and other constables found Andrews sleeping on a sofa and Raymond Stevens sleeping in a child's cot. In a wardrobe they found a pistol. Garlepp said "I wouldn't turn them out. They came here from Pentridge and I let them stay." She admitted that she received sustenance at the rate of 6/ a week and also received 8/ a week from the Children's Welfare department for her child.

For the defence of Andrews bank correspondence was produced showing that he was in receipt of a remittance from England. He was discharged.

Garlepp convicted and sentenced to imprisonment for three months, but an order was made suspending the sentence upon Garlepp entering a bond of £20 to be of good behaviour for a year. She was also convicted on a charge of having being in possession of an unregistered pistol, and was fined £1. An order was made for the confiscation of the weapon.

Norman Stevens and Raymond Stevens, who both admitted previous convictions, were each sentenced to imprisonment for three months.

Henry (Heinrich) Garlepp	1861-1916
married	1886
Catherine French	1858–1925
children	
Ellen Garlepp	1887–1942
married	1907
James Spencer Harnden	1884–1972
children	
Ellen Kathleen Harnden	1908–1961
married	1933
Robert Alexander Whitten	1906–1976
children	
Patricia Agnes Whitten	1937–2015
James Henry Spencer Harnden	1910–1972
married	1936
Bessie Laura Elizbeth Wallace	1916–1995
William Edward Harnden	1912–1936
Agnes Harnden	1915–1988
married	1935
Albert Keith Strong	1913–1967
children	
George William Strong	1936–2010
George Patrick Harnden	1918–1987
married	
Norreen Phyllis May McDonald	
Harry Harnden	1920–1995
married	1943
Myrtle Dora Sposito	1924–2009
John Joseph Harnden	1922–2004
married	
Gweneth Evylin May McDonald	1927–1984
Edward Harnden	1924–1999
Ellen Mary Harnden	1926–2002
married	1947
Keith Desmond Cowen	1923–2011
married	1962
Jeremiah Dempsey	1922–2005
Patricia Nancy Harnden	1928–2013
married	1947
Leslie George Jackson	
children	
Anette Petrita Jackson	–1957

Raymond Johnathon Bettess	
Ernest Spencer Harnden	1930–2016
married	1950
Betty Loraine Shaw	1934–1998
children	
Michael Shane Harnden	1956–1956
Katherine Harnden	
Kathleen Garlepp	1889–1956
married	1910
James William Little	1892–1964
children	
James William Henry Little	1911–1952
married	1943
Ellen Mary O'Farrell	1915–1967
Nellie Veneta Little	1912–1982
married	1937
Russell William Michael Green	
Harold James "Joe" Meehan	1911–1967
George Patrick Garlepp	1891–1954
married	1914
Grace Louise Shore	1895–1953
children	
Edith May Garlepp	1914–1914
William Roy Garlepp	1915–1998
married	1938
Ivy May Wiles	1915–1969
Edward Patrick Garlepp	1917–1974
George Patrick Garlepp	1918–1978
married	1942
Jessie Stewart Ousley	1921–1968
children	
Trevor Russell Garlepp	1943–2004
Noeline Helen Garlepp	1945–2016
married	about 1951
Margaret May	1916–1981
Kathleen Mary Garlepp	1920–1980
married	1942
Patrick Joseph Meehan	1922–1969
children	
John Patrick Meehan	1947–1977
Brian Meehan	1948–1989
Peter Anthony Meehan	1957–1991
Dianne Marie Meehan	–1955

Agnes "Pat" Garlepp	1925–2000
married	1946
Cyril Wallace English	1921–1993
John Patrick Garlepp	1928–1955
Mary Garlepp	1894–1894
Henry Garlepp	1894–1904
Mary Agnes Garlepp	1898–1961
married	1926
Sidney Seymour Shore	1897–1971
children	
Sidney Edward Shore	1928–2019
Edward Garlepp	1901–1931
married	1922
Sophia Agnes Smith	1902-1968
children	
Nancy	
married	1951
Allan Richard Wood	

Ernest Garlepp

Ernest Garlepp was my 2 x great Grandfather. He was born 24 June, 1864 in Somerton Victoria. His was the youngest child of Carl Friedrich Wilhelm (Charles) Garlepp Sr (1817–1886) and Elizabeth Cornelia Garlepp (nee Brauer 1821–1941). I have attached a copy of his birth certificate on the following page.

On 2 May, 1884, when Ernest was 19 years old, he married Ellen French (1866-1931) in the St Joseph's Church, Benalla, Victoria. I have attached a copy of the certificate on the following page.

Ellen was the 5th child of John French (1833-1917) and Ellen O'Halloran (1833-1903). She was also the sister of Catherine French (1858-1925) who married Ernest's brother, Henry (1861-1916) and Sarah Ann French (1867-1935) who married Ernest's brother, William (1856-?).

Ernest and Ellen lived in the Tamleugh area when they first married and Ernest was working as a labourer.

On 27 June, 1884, their first child was born , Charles Henry in Violet Town, Victoria
On 28 March, 1886 Ernest Edward was born in Baddaginnie, Victoria
Mary Ellen was born in 1889 in Yarrawonga.

The family then moved the suburbs of Melbourne, where
Ethel Maude was born 17 June, 1891 in Port Melbourne and
John Joseph was born 5 December, 1895 in Port Melbourne.

SCHEDULE A.

SCHEDULE B.

BIRTHS in the District of _____ in the Colony

In the Colony of Victoria.

[COUNTERPART.]

SCHEDULE D.—28 VICT. No. 268,

CERTIFICATE OF MARRIAGE.

District _of Benalla_ .... No. in Register _65_

On _2nd May_ 1884 ...... at _St Josephs Church Benalla_

Marriage _by licence_ .... was solemnized between Us according to the

Rites of the Catholic Church

Signature ...... _Ernest Garlepp_

DESCRIPTION.	Residence { Present	_Tanneuff_
	{ Usual	_Tanneuff_
	Age _21_	
	Rank or Profession	_Labour_
	Condition	_Bachelor_
	If Widower { Former Wife } Deceased in	{ Children ...... { Living ...... Dead ......
	Birth Place	_Tanneuff_
	Parents' Names and { Father	_Charles Garlepp Farmer_
	Rank or Profession { Mother (Maiden Surname.)	_Elizabeth Brawner_

Signature ...... _Ellen French_

DESCRIPTION.	Residence { Present	_Tanneuff_
	{ Usual	_Tanneuff_
	Age _21_	
	Rank or Profession	_Lady_
	Condition	_Spinster_
	If Widow { Former Husband } Deceased in	{ Children ...... { Living ...... Dead ......
	Birth Place	_New S Wales_
	Parents' Names and { Father	_John French Farmer_
	Rank or Profession { Mother (Maiden Surname.)	_Ellen O'Halloran_

I, ... _Patrick _____ being a Cath Clergyman_

do hereby certify that I have this day at _St Josephs Church Benalla_

duly celebrated Marriage between _Ernest Garlepp_

...... and _Ellen French_

...... after notice and declaration duly made and published as by law required.

Dated this _2nd_ ...... day of _May_ ...... 1884.

Signature of Minister, Registrar-General, or other officer. ......

Witnesses { _William _____ _Kate French_ }

139

On 12 September, 1896, in was reported in The Argus that Ernest was living in Ben Nevis Street, Heathcote, working as a line repairer and had become financially Insolvent. (see Below left) This was a time of depression in Victoria and many people found themselves in court for insolvency.   This must have been a very stressful time for Edward and Ellen, with their young family. The article, below right was found in The McIvor Times and Rodney Advertiser on 24 September, 1896.

NEW INSOLVENTS.

Ernest Garlepp, of Ben Nevis-street, Heathcote, line repairer. Liabilities, £62 0s. 6d.; assets, £3 ; deficiency, £59 0s. 6d. Filed at Heathcote.

Peter O'Loghlen, of Toborac, railway employe. Liabilities, £52 11s. 6d.; assets, £7 ; deficiency, £45 11s. 6d. Filed at Heathcote.

Joseph Davis, of Jersey-villa, Raleigh-street, St. Kilda, formerly jam manufacturer, now out of business. Causes of insolvency—Compulsory sequestration of the estate of Davis and Co., of which insolvent was a member, and want of sufficient capital. Liabilities, nil ; assets, £27 13s.; surplus, £27 13s. Mr. T. J. Davey, trustee of estate of Davis and Company.

William Linton, of Maryborough, hospital dispenser. Causes of insolvency—Smallness of income, pressure of creditors, and losses in mining, breeding poultry, &c. Liabilities, £55 15s. 6d.; assets, £1 10s.; deficiency, £54

In the Court of Insolvency, Heathcote.

NOTICE is hereby given that the Estates of Ernest Garlepp of Ben Nevis Street, Heathcote, line repairer, and Peter O'Loghlen of Touborac, railway employe, have been sequestrated, and that General Meetings of Creditors in the said Estates will be hoiden at the Insolvency Court Offices at Heathcote on Friday, the 25th day of September, A.D. 1896, at the hour of eleven o'clock in the forenoon, for the Election of Trustees and for the other purposes mentioned in the 53rd section of the Insolvency Act 1890.

Dated at Heathcote this 11th day of September, A.D. 1896.

W. T. TONKS,
Chief Clerk.

Ernest Garlepp applied for a certificate of discharge. Liabilities, £66 ; Assets, £3. Causes of insolvency, sickness of himself and family. Granted. Mr Murphy made the applications in this and the previous case.

According to a report in The McIvor Times and Rodney Advertiser on 6 May, 1897, Ernest had applied for certificate of discharge.

In 1897, Ernest was fined for not sending his daughter, Mary to school. The picture below is an excerpt from the court records.

In 1898, Ernest and Ellen are living in Montrose Street, Hawthorn.

On 25 May, 1899, Kate was born in Hawthorn and on 21 June, 1902 Lily Agnes was born in Brunswick.

In 1903 they were living at 40 Brunswick Road, Brunswick and Ernest was working as a gatekeeper.

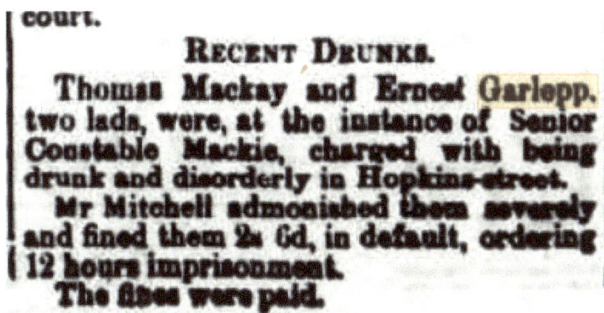

court.

RECENT DRUNKS.

Thomas Mackay and Ernest Garlepp, two lads, were, at the instance of Senior Constable Mackie, charged with being drunk and disorderly in Hopkins-street.

Mr Mitchell admonished them severely and fined them 2s 6d, in default, ordering 12 hours imprisonment.

The fines were paid.

Ernest was charged with being drunk and disorderly, in June 1905 and was fined 2s 6d.

The article was found in The Independent on 3 June 1905.

Unfortunately for Ernest he again found himself insolvent. The article to the right was found in the Argus on 2 August, 1906. It says that Ernest was now living in Victoria Street, Footscray, working as a gateman. He stated that the cause of his insolvency was, loss of salary, sickness in family and pressure of creditors.

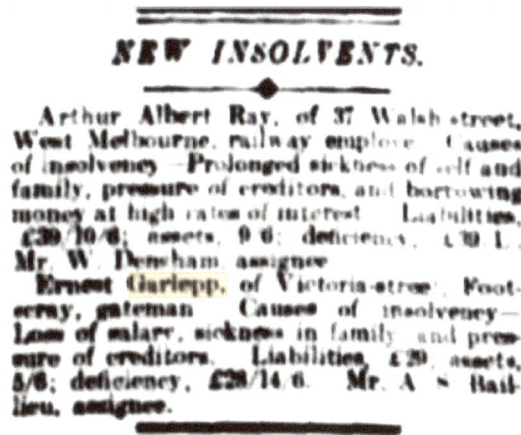

NEW INSOLVENTS.

Arthur Albert Ray, of 37 Walsh-street, West Melbourne, railway employe Causes of insolvency Prolonged sickness of self and family, pressure of creditors, and borrowing money at high rates of interest. Liabilities, £39/10/6; assets, 9 6; deficiency, £39 1. Mr. W. Densham assignee

Ernest Garlepp, of Victoria-street, Footscray, gateman Causes of insolvency— Loss of salary, sickness in family and pressure of creditors. Liabilities, £29, assets, 5/6; deficiency, £28/14 6. Mr. A S Baillieu, assignee.

In 1909, the family are now living at 196 Barkers Road, Hawthorn and Ernest is working as a Railway Man.

In 1918, Ernest is living in Frankston and working a line repairer. The following year, in 1918, Ellen and Ernest move to Yatpool, near Mildura, where Ernest works as a Railway Ganger. They seemed to have stayed there until Ernest retired and they to Pakenham where they lived with their Daughter, Mary and her family. On 7 August, 1931, Ellen died in the St Vincent's Hospital, Melbourne.

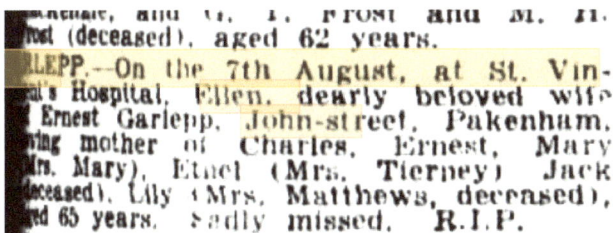

...chair, and t., 1., Frost and M. H. Frost (deceased), aged 62 years.

GARLEPP.—On the 7th August, at St. Vincent's Hospital, Ellen, dearly beloved wife of Ernest Garlepp, John-street, Pakenham, loving mother of Charles, Ernest, Mary (Mrs. Mary), Ethel (Mrs. Tierney) Jack (deceased), Lily (Mrs. Matthews, deceased), aged 65 years. Sadly missed. R.I.P.

Ernest Died on 19th November, 1936. His death certificate is shown below where it states he died from heart failure.

THIRD SCHEDULE.

10841

DEATHS in the District of MELBOURNE, in Victoria, Registered by SAMUEL HENRY EDGERTON HOLLOW.

1 No.	10841
Description—	
2 When and where died	19th. November, 1936, Nazareth House, Cornell Street, East Camberwell, City of Camberwell, County of Bourke. U.R. Unknown.
3 Name and surname	Ernest GARLEPP,
Occupation	Ganger (Railways).
4 Sex and age	Male, 72 years.
5 (1) Cause of death	Heart failure — some months,
(2) Duration of last illness	Emphysema and
(3) Legally qualified medical practitioner by whom certified ... and	chronic bronchitis) — several years, Dr. J.E.Mahon,
(4) When he last saw deceased ...	4th November, 1936.
6 Name and surname of father and mother (maiden name, if known), with occupation	Ernest Garlepp, Elizabeth Garlepp, formerly Brewer, Hotelkeeper.
7 Signature, description, and residence of informant	*[signature]* Authorized Agent, Racecourse Road, North Melbourne.
8 (1) Signature of Registrar ...	*[signature]*
(2) Date	10th December, 1936. Melbourne.
(3) Where registered	
If burial registered—	
9 When and where buried ...	21st. November, 1936, Berwick Cemetery, A. V. Tobin acting for A. V. Tobin Proprietary Limited.
Undertaker by whom certified ...	
10 Name and religion of Minister, or names of witnesses of burial ...	J. Morice, R. G. Smith.
11 Where born, and how long in the Australian States, stating which	Somerton, Victoria, 72 years in Victoria.
If deceased was married—	
12 (1) Where ... ... and	Benalla, Victoria,
(2) At what age ... ... and	20 years,
(3) To whom	Ellen French.
13 Issue in order of birth, the names and ages	Charles, 52 years, Ernest, 50 years, Mary Ellen, 47 years, Ethel Maud, 45 years, John Joseph, deceased, Kate, 37 years, Lily Agnes, deceased. ... ...

N.882/0.55.—10377.

10841

142

Charles Henry Garlepp (1884-1949), the eldest child of Ernest and Ellen was born 27 June, 1884 in Violet Town Victoria.

In 1907 he married Clara Maud Harnden (1888-1982) in Richmond Victoria. Clara was the sister of James Spencer Harnden (1884-1972), who married Ellen Garlepp (1887-1942), Charles' cousin.

Clara was born 28 August, 1888 in Richmond she was the daughter of Henry Colins Harnden (1857-1894) and Mary Jane (nee Thornton (1862-1915).

Charles and Clara were living at 30 Kelvin Place, Auburn in 1909.
In 1914 they were living 6 Milton Place, Richmond South.

Charles and Clara had the following children:

John Joseph Garlepp	1909–2000
Ivy Agnes Garlepp	1910–after 1980
Ernest Edward Garlepp	1912–1914
Charles Henry Garlepp	1912–1913
Leslie Michael Garlepp	1918–1987

Two of their children died in infancy. They placed the following notice in The Age on 20 February, 1913

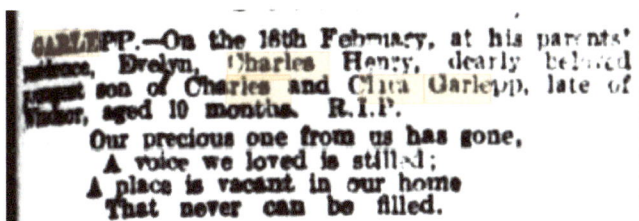

GARLEPP.—On the 16th February, at his parents'
residence, Evelyn, Charles Henry, dearly beloved
son of Charles and Clara Garlepp, late of
Windsor, aged 10 months. R.I.P.
Our precious one from us has gone,
A voice we loved is stilled;
A place is vacant in our home
That never can be filled.

In 1924 the family was living in Langs Road, Ivanhoe and Charles was working as a labourer.

In 1937 the family were now living at 1 Minona Street, Hawthorn where Charles is working as a labourer.

In 1942 Charles and Clara were living in a flat at 389 Punt Road, Richmond.

He was employed as a storeman.

Charles died on 23 January, 1949 at the age of 64. He died at their son, William Patricks home at 185 Kilby road, East Kew. He was buried in the Carlton North Cemetery. The family inserted the notice in The Argus on 24 January, 1949.

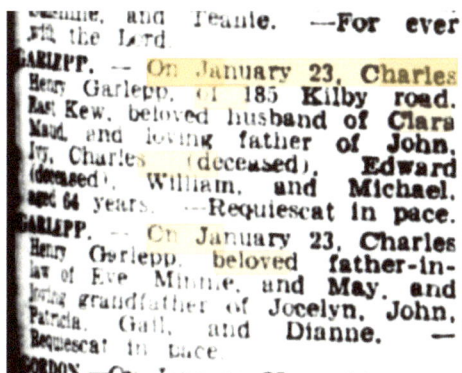

Clara died in Queensland on 6 June, 1982 at the age of 93. Ivy was living in Queensland at the time, so I assume Clara either had moved in with her or was on holiday when she died. Her body was returned to Melbourne and she was buried in The Carlton North Cemetery.

John Joseph Garlepp, Charles and Clara's eldest child was born 10 October, 1909 in Richmond, Victoria.

In1933 John married Eve Christine Stubbs (1908-1989)

John and Eve had the following children:

Jocelyn Garlepp	1934–
John Garlepp	1936–
Diane Garlepp	1947–
Michael Charles Garlepp	1956–

From around 1947 to 1950 John and his sister Ivy were conducting a business called Garlepp Manufacturing and Wendy Lou Fashions. There are quite a lot of advertisements published looking for employees. It seems to be a dress making business with shop outlets.

The article to the right, from The Age 1 March, 1950, shows that Ivy gave over the operations of the business to John.

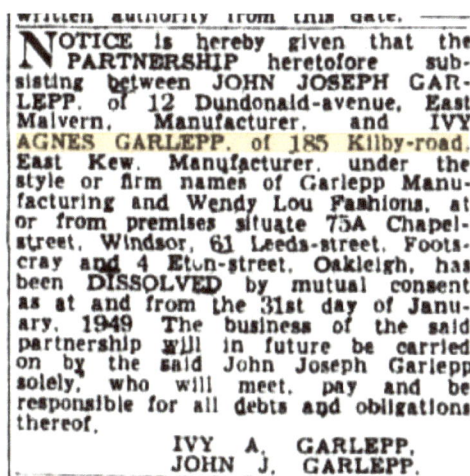

written authority from this date. —
NOTICE is hereby given that the PARTNERSHIP heretofore subsisting between JOHN JOSEPH GARLEPP, of 12 Dundonald-avenue, East Malvern, Manufacturer, and IVY AGNES GARLEPP, of 185 Kilby-road, East Kew. Manufacturer, under the style or firm names of Garlepp Manufacturing and Wendy Lou Fashions, at or from premises situate 75A Chapel-street, Windsor, 61 Leeds-street, Footscray and 4 Eton-street, Oakleigh, has been DISSOLVED by mutual consent as at and from the 31st day of January, 1949 The business of the said partnership will in future be carried on by the said John Joseph Garlepp solely, who will meet, pay and be responsible for all debts and obligations thereof.

IVY A. GARLEPP,
JOHN J. GARLEPP.

In 1954 John and Eve are farming on "Kelvin Park" Longwarry, Victoria. They moved from there to another farm at Nar Nar Goon, Victoria, which is shown on the electoral rolls.

Here are a couple of advertisement in the newspapers about the sale of the farms.

Lilydale farm £68/10/acre

A dairy farm of 393 acres at Lilydale was sold at auction yesterday for £26,920/10/.

The property fronts the main Lilydale - Healesville road, about three miles from the town. Improvements include a brick house and dairy buildings.

Bidding opened at £50 an acre, and several buyers carried it to £68/10. Buyer was Mr. J. J. Garlepp, of Longwarry. Vendor was Mrs. L. C. Onley.

Gippsland and Northern Co. Ltd. were the auctioneer.

melbourne.

APPLICATION for TRANSFER of LICENCE.—I, William Duncan, of 375 Inkerman street, St. Kilda, hotel keeper, the holder of a Victualler's licence for Inkerman Hotel, at 375 Inkerman street, St. Kilda, in the Southern Metropolitan Licensing Area, and we, John Joseph Garlepp, Eve Christina Garlepp, and John Barry Garlepp, all of 32 Commercial road, Prahran, hereby give notice that we will APPLY to the Licensing Court at Melbourne on Monday, the 4th day of July, 1955, for the TRANSFER of the LICENCE to the said John Joseph Garlepp, on behalf of himself and the said Eve Christina Garlepp and John Barry Garlepp, trading in partnership under the style or firm of J. J., E. C., and J. B. Garlepp.

Dated the 24th day of June, 1955.

W DUNCAN
J. J. GARLEPP
EVE C. GARLEPP
JOHN B. GARLEPP

Messrs Hedderwick, Fookes & Alston, 103 William street, Melbourne, solicitors for the transferor.

Keith A. Ness, 411 Collins street, Melbourne, solicitor for the transferees.

H. B. LARSEN, 8 Albion street, St. Kilda, Hotel Broker.

WEDNESDAY, MARCH 17, 11 a.m.

On the Property, Prince's Highway

PICNIC POINT, LONGWARRY

A/c. W. P. GARLEPP, Esq.

HIGHLY PRODUCTIVE RIVER FRONTAGE DAIRY FARM

ALEX. SCOTT & CO. PTY. LTD. and J. J. KAVANAGH, Garfield (Agents in conjunction), have been favored with instructions to submit to Auction as above, the well-known property, "WATTLE VALLEY FARM," on Prince's Highway, Longwarry, next "Picnic Point" Reserve, 5 miles Drouin, 54 miles Melbourne.

LAND consists of 147 acres of undulating rises and rich black flats, all under very good pasture, except approximately five acres cult. and shelter timber.

IMPROVEMENTS include one of the most comfortable homesteads in the district, with S.E.C. and tel. connected; 9 rooms, with every modern convenience, including el. h.w.s., stove, built-in cupboards, etc. ALSO Manager's cottage of 4 rooms with S.E.C. connected. COWSHED is particularly well designed, 8 bails for milking, and add. 16 feed stalls; S.E.C. power and el. hot water service, and also ext. tel. to house. Very large concrete yards and ramps; 2 feed sheds; big hay shed; imp. shed; tool shed—all in excellent order. New brick calf shed and paddock.

FENCING: Subdivided into 22 paddocks, all fencing is in first-class condition.

WATER is a feature of the property, having approx. one mile frontage to the Tarago River, from which water is pumped to house, garden, sheds, and all the paddocks, with 10,000 gallon brick storage tank, situated on highest point of the farm, giving a particularly good pressure.

REMARKS: This is an outstanding dairy farm, easily handled, and with every modern conv., which will show high returns from the day of possession. Prior to Mr. Garlepp, was in the hands of the Lilley family for 40 years. Very well laid out, with a lane through the centre of property giving access to all paddocks. Would lend itself very readily to spray irrigation. A milk contract of 80 gallons per day can be taken over, and it should be further noted that the average of Mr. Garlepp's herd exceeds £90 per head per annum. Mr. Garlepp wishes to go back into business and is determined to sell. State School, E. High School and Convent School buses pass gate.

TERMS: £1000 deposit on signing contract, balance on possession within 30 days. Good finance available. Please contact agents prior to date of sale.

VENDOR'S SOLICITOR: Keith A. Ness, 411 Collins Street, Melbourne, C.1.

PROPERTY WILL BE OFFERED AT 11 O'CLOCK

Also—

IMMEDIATELY FOLLOWING :

CLEARANCE SALE of COMPLETE STOCK and PLANT, including :—

STOCK:
61 PICKED MILKING COWS (mostly Friesians; various stages).
8 HEIFERS (2½ years), mostly Friesians; calve September).
5 HEIFERS (12 months).
8 HEIFER CALVES (3 to 6 months).
2 BULLS (1 reg. Guernsey, 1 Friesian, 3 years).
1 REG. FRIESIAN BULL (6 months).
1 HORSE (all work).

The above cattle are all T.B. tested, mostly young, in full production, and are one of the top herds in the Bunyip Herd Test Association. The young stock are all from picked cows, and extra good.

PLANT Includes:
Ferguson Tractor (12 months old and in perfect order, with over-size tyres and light and foot plates, and following attachments: Side Delivery Rake, Sub-soiler, Blade Terracer, Belt-pulley, Jack. International 6-ft. Power Mower. Morris Commercial Truck (done 19,000 miles, in perfect order). Crump Manure Spreader (near brand new). Six-unit Royal Medal Milking Machines; Cooler; Vat and Fittings; El. Motor; Separator with El. Motor (as new); 17 Milk Cans; Cement Mixer; Chaffcutter; Tractor Trailer; Car Trailer; Cart Trailer; Hay Bale Elevator; Rake; Sweep; 2 Ploughs; 3-leaf Cult. Harrows; Grass Harrows; Disc Harrows (4' 6"); Scuffler; Leveller; Pulper; Grinder; Saw Bench; Scoop; Qty. Posts; Concrete Brick Machine (new); Qty. 44-gallon Drums; 2000 Bales Good Grass Hay. Also Small Items and Sundries too numerous to mention.

LUNCHEON AVAILABLE. LOADING RACE & TRANSPORT.

Further details, or appointment to inspect property, apply:

J. J. KAVANAGH — GARFIELD.

TEL. IONA 214—OR

ALEX. SCOTT & CO. PTY. LTD.

WARRAGUL & DANDENONG—Tel. Warragul 31.

From the notice shown to the right, from the Argus, 25 June 1955, John and Eve and their son John Barry applied for a Licence for the Inkerman Hotel in St Kilda.

From the 1958 Electoral Rolls, John Barry is a Hotel Manager, and I assume he was still running the Inkerman.

Above is a picture of the Inkerman, taken in 2004.

In 1967 John is working as an Investor and he and Eve are living at 58 Alfred Street, Kew.

In 1977 John and Eve are living at 3 Kyila Court Frankston.

On 1 June, 1989 at the age of 81, Eve died. She was cremated at the Springvale Crematorium.

On 7 January, 2000 at the age of 90, John died at the Tandera Hostel. He was cremated at the Springvale Crematorium. I found this notice from Jocelyn.

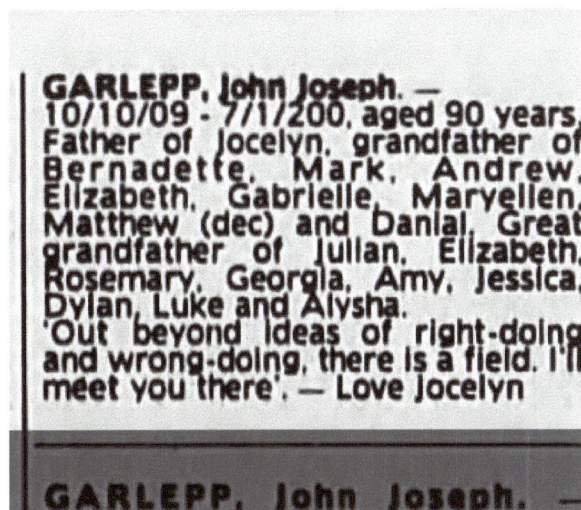

GARLEPP, John Joseph. — 10/10/09 - 7/1/200, aged 90 years, Father of Jocelyn, grandfather of Bernadette, Mark, Andrew, Elizabeth, Gabrielle, Maryellen, Matthew (dec) and Danial. Great grandfather of Julian, Elizabeth, Rosemary, Georgia, Amy, Jessica, Dylan, Luke and Alysha. 'Out beyond ideas of right-doing and wrong-doing, there is a field. I'll meet you there'. — Love Jocelyn

GARLEPP, John Joseph. —

Ivy Agnes Garlepp was born in 1911 and was the second child of Charles and Clara Garlepp.

Ivy married Leslie Richard Burton (1917-1995) in 1943. The relationship does not seem to have lasted many years and the two parted. I cannot find any divorce but Ivy resumed her maiden name. As mentioned earlier Ivy and John, her brother were running a business. After this was wound up in 1850, Ivy partnered with Lindsay William Deppeler (1919-1980) and took his name, although I have not found a marriage registered.

Lindsay's family owned the historic Lynnburn estate in Batesford. The Deppeler's were famous for their vineyards and wines. Ivy and Lindsay were living there in 1854 when it was sold. I have a picture of the advertisement on the next page.

"Lynnburn"

This advertisement appeared in The Weekly Times on 24 March 1954,

149

The advertisement to the right was in the Argus on 2 April, 1949. Ivy applied for a Licence for the Royal Mail Hotel at Diamond Creek.

The advertisement below was in the Argus on 5 July 1952. Ivy had transferred the licence to C. Fisher.

The Royal Mail,
Diamond Creek.

On 19 June, 1954, Ivy and Lindsay bought the Hotel Max, in commercial Road, Prahran.

The two articles below were found in The Argus, 19 June, 1954.

Hotel Max sold

The Hotel Max, Commercial rd., Prahran, has been sold on account of Mr. J. A. McInerney to Mr. and Mrs. L. W. Deppeler, of Batesford, for an undisclosed price. Brokers were Michael Grant and Co.

Collins street, Melbourne.

APPLICATION for TRANSFER of LICENCE. I Margaret Edith Christie the holder of a Victualler's licence for the Max Hotel at Commercial road, Prahran, in the Prahran Licensing District, and we, Ivy Agnes Deppeler and Lindsay William Deppeler both of Batesford, via Geelong hereby give notice that we will APPLY to the Licensing Court at Melbourne on Monday, the 28th day of June 1954, for the TRANSFER of the LICENCE to the said Ivy Agnes Deppeler, on behalf of herself and the said Lindsay William Deppeler, trading in partnership as "I. A. & L. W. Deppeler."
Dated the 17th day of June 1954.
MARGARET EDITH CHRISTIE,
Transferor.
I. A. DEPPELER {
L. DEPPELER {
Transferees.
Brendan McGuinness & Co., 351 Little Collins st., Melbourne, solicitors for the transferor.
Bernard Nolan, 383 Bourke st., Melbourne, solicitor for the transferees.
Mahony, O'Brien & Duggan, 31 Queen st., Melbourne, solicitors for the vendors.
MICHAEL GRANT & Co. Hotel Brokers, Auctioneers, Agents & Valuers, 114 Queen st., Melbourne MU6641.

A APPLICATION for TRANSFER

I am unsure when Ivy and Lindsay sold the Hotel Max, but around 1970 they had moved to Queensland. In 1972 they were living at 1 Old Burleigh Road, Surfers Paradise. In 1980 they had moved to a unit at 12a/21 Armrick Avenue, Broadbeach, Queensland.

I have no information of the couple after that. I cannot find their deaths registered.

William Patrick Garlepp was the 5th child of Charles and Clara Garlepp. He was born around 1915 in Melbourne, Victoria. When Patrick was about 23 he married Minnie Elsie Hansen (1915-2004). Minnie was the daughter of John and Elsie Hansen. The below article was found in the Age on 23 July, 1938.

Lovely Veil of Honiton Lace

ST. JOHN'S CHURCH, EAST MALVERN, was the setting for a
very pretty wedding recently, when Miss Minnie Elsie Hansen,
younger daughter of Mr. J. Hansen, of Murrumbeena, and the
late Mrs. Hansen, was married to Mr. William Patrick Garlepp, son
son of Mr. and Mrs. C. Garlepp, of Minona-street, Auburn.

The bride chose a gown of ivory satin, made on tailored lines, with
a high-cut bodice softly gathered into the moulded waist-line. The full
skirt was cut on the bias, to fall into a circular train at the back. Her
veil of lovely Honiton lace, lent by her sister, Mrs. Mellords, was worn
on layers of tulle, and held in place by a coronet of opalescent beads.
She carried a bouquet of deep cream gladioli and begonias.

Shell-pink brocaded satin fashioned the frock and jacket worn by the
only bridesmaid, Miss Brenda Jones. A tulle veil in the same delicate
shade was worn over her hair, falling from a coronet of pink tinted flowers. A bouquet of deep pink gladioli and begonias was carried.

Mr. John Garlepp, brother of the groom, supported him as best man.
Later a reception was held at the Central Park Kiosk, where pink and
flowers decorated the tables.

— Mendelssohn

152

In 1942, William was a 'rubber worker' and he and Elsie were living at 2 Maroora Street, Malvern East.

In 1949, William and Elsie were living at 185 Kilby Road, Kew North and Elsie's occupation is described as manufacturer and Bill is a 'traveller'.

In 1954, William applied for a Licence for the Princes Highway Hotel, Pakenham.

Bona fide change stirs hotels

TRADE WILL FIGHT SUNDAY BAN

TWO hours after State Cabinet decided yesterday to restrict Sunday hotel drinking to meal hours, the U.L.V.A. announced it would fight the plan.

Cabinet agreed to abolish the present bone fide Sunday traveller law.

This means that motorists will obtain a drink on Sundays only if they eat at an hotel.

Liquor will be served with meals between noon and 2.30 p.m. and between 6 p.m. and 10 p.m.

The change has to be ratified by the Parliamentary L.C.P., which meets today.

The U.L.V.A. claims the revision restricts public liberties and penalises freedom of the travelling public because of the irresponsible behavior of a few.

Mr. Rylah, Chief Secretary, said abolition of the bona-fide law was the only way of meeting the menace of all-day drinking on Sundays.

This drinking had led to dangerous driving, with its consequent loss of life, and to the invasion of country towns outside the 20-mile radius by people, who took over towns on Sundays for drinking, he said.

Mr. K. Corridon, U.L.V.A general secretary, said last night

Only 3.3%

"We state very firmly on behalf of the bona-fide traveller on the roads on Sundays that on police figures only 3.3% of road accidents are due to drink.

"This proposal will deny the bona-fide traveller from Charlton to Swan Hill having a drink on a hot Sunday, merely because the Government is concerned that some people have a drink after travelling 20 miles from Melbourne."

"Sly grog"

Country hotelkeepers condemned Cabinet's decision forecast it would open up a new era in "sly grog," with no reduction in Sunday drinking.

"If a person wants to drink on Sunday he will. This decision, if approved, will mean they will drink in uncontrolled, unhealthy conditions," said a leading hotelier.

Individual comments last night were:

Bill Garlepp, licensee, Princes Highway Hotel, Pakenham: "The decision paves the way to create the most chaotic state Victoria has known. It will lead to black marketing and

J. S. Coventry, licensee, Golden Fleece Hotel, Melton: "Last Sunday a sports team held a picnic in the park here and got through more beer than the two hotels served."

more beer than the two hotels served."

F. Gooda, licensee, Pier Hotel, Frankston: "Instead of drinking in hotels, people will hold parties on the beaches. With summer approaching, people naturally drink more."

The Argus 11 October 1955

154

By 1972, William and Elsie had moved to 51 Jasper Crescent Frankston and he has no occupation on the electoral rolls.

In 1980, when William was 65 he had moved to Queensland with Elsie and they were living at 13 Conifer Crescent Cypress Gardens.

Nothing more is known about William, I cannot find his death registration.

Elsie moved back to Victoria and was living in the Wangaratta Nursing home where she died on 4 January, 2004 at the age of 91.

> Minnie Garlepp Obituary
>
> Published by Legacy Remembers on Jan. 13, 2004.
>
> GARLEPP. - Minnie Elsie, passed away peacefully at Wangaratta Nursing Home (Dicker Wing) on Sunday, Jan. 4, 2004 aged 91 years. Beloved wife of Bill (dec.), dearly loved aunt of Elsie and Charles, Wesley and Judy, Janice and Roy, Sylvia and Tony (dec.). Loved great aunt of their families. At rest with her beloved Bill

Leslie Michael Garlepp was the youngest child of Charles and Clara Garlepp. He was born 12 April, 1918 when his parents were living at 16 Haines Street, Hawthorn.

When Leslie was 22 he enlisted in the Armed Forces.

B

MEDICAL EXAMINATION

I have made full and careful examination of the abovenamed person in accordance with the instructions contained in the Standing Orders for Australian Army Medical Services. In my opinion he is—*

1. Fit for Class I.

2. ~~Temporarily unfit for Class I~~ †

3. ~~Fit for Class II.~~

4. ~~Temporarily unfit for Class II~~ †

5. ~~Unfit for military service~~ †

Place................FOOTSCRAY.. Date.............15.8.40

Signature of Examining Medical Officer ....

* Classifications which are inapplicable to be struck out.   † Reasons for unfitness to be stated.

C

OATH OF ENLISTMENT ‡

For persons voluntarily enlisted or called upon under Part III. or Part IV. of the Defence Act to serve in the Citizen Forces in time of war. Not compulsory for serving members of the Forces or those allotted to the Citizen Forces under Part XII. of the Act, but unless in any case an objection is raised, the oath should be administered to them as part of the ceremony of attestation.

I, *Leslie Garlepp* ....swear that I will well and truly serve our Sovereign Lord, the King, in the Military Forces of the Commonwealth of Australia until the cessation of the present time of war or until sooner lawfully discharged, dismissed, or removed, and that I will resist His Majesty's enemies and cause His Majesty's peace to be kept and maintained, and that I will in all matters appertaining to my service faithfully discharge my duty according to law.

So Help Me God! ‡‡‡

Signature of Person Enlisted......*L Garlepp.*

Subscribed at.......FOOTSCRAY...........................in the State of....VICTORIA

this..........16th...........................day of......*August*......................19 40

Before me—

Signature of Attesting Officer......................................*E D... Smith Capt*
A.O. 32A

‡ Persons who object to take an oath may make an affirmation in accordance with the Third Schedule of the Defence Act. In such case the above form will be amended accordingly and initialled by the Attesting Officer.

VX100612

Victorian Railways Printing Works, North Melbourne.

VX 100612

AUSTRALIAN MILITARY FORCES.

A.A. Form A.200.
(Revised April, 1941.)

ATTESTATION FORM.

FOR SPECIAL FORCES RAISED FOR SERVICE IN AUSTRALIA OR ABROAD.

Army No. V75266

Surname GARLEPP. (BLOCK CAPITALS) .... Other Names Leslie

Unit B.1.P.O.D.

Enlisted for service at BROADMEADOWS. (Place)

VICTORIA (State) 6ᵈ September 1942 (Date)

A. Questions to be put to persons called out or presenting themselves for voluntary enlistment.

1.	What is your name?	1.	Surname GARLEPP. (BLOCK CAPITALS) Other names Leslie
2.	Where were you born?	2.	In or near the town of Glenfurrie in the State or country of Victoria, Australia.
3.	Are you a natural born or a naturalized British Subject? If the latter, papers are to be produced	3.	Natural Born
4.	What is your age and date of birth?	4.	Age 24 years. Date of Birth 12ᵗʰ April 1918
5.	What is your trade or occupation?	5.	Machinist (Engineering)
6.	Are you married, single or widower?	6.	Married
7.	Give details of previous Military Service	7.	A.M.F. No. V75266 Rank Sgt. Unit 120ᵈ RMT coy OTHER MILITARY SERVICE No. V75266 Rank Pte Unit 13 Sup Pers Coy
8.	If now serving, give particulars	8.	No. 75266 Rank Sgt. Unit B.1.P.O.D. RASC
9.	Who is your actual next of kin? (Order of relationship:—wife, eldest son, eldest daughter, father, mother, eldest brother, eldest sister, eldest half-brother, eldest half-sister.)	9.	Name Mrs M. Garlepp Address 25 Smith St St Kilda Victoria Relationship Wife
10.	What is your permanent address?	10.	25 Smith St St Kilda Victoria
11.	What is your religious denomination? (Answer optional.)	11.	R.C.
12.	Have you ever been convicted by a civil court?	12.	No
13.	Have you any of the following Educational Qualifications? If so, which?		1. Certificate for Entry to Secondary School Merit. 2. Intermediate 3. Leaving 4. Leaving Honours 5. Technical Caulfield Tec Sch. 1½ yrs 6. University Degrees 7. Other Diplomas

I, Leslie Garlepp do solemnly declare that the above answers made by me to the above questions are true and that I am willing to serve in the Australian Military Forces within or beyond the limits of the Commonwealth.

Witnessed by Kar Bradley Major
(Signature of Attesting or Witnessing Officer)

L Garlepp
(Signature)

* The person will be warned that should he give false answers to any of these questions he will be liable to heavy penalties under the Defence Act.

B. MEDICAL EXAMINATION

I certify the above-named person to be fit for Class as per Don 3/6/42. Temporarily unfit.

Unfit
Octobber Lieut (Signature)

C. OATH OF ENLISTMENT †

I, Leslie Garlepp swear that I will well and truly serve our Sovereign Lord, the King, in the Military Forces of the Commonwealth of Australia until the cessation of the present time of war and twelve months thereafter or until sooner lawfully discharged, dismissed or removed, and that I will resist His Majesty's enemies and cause His Majesty's peace to be kept and maintained, and that I will in all matters appertaining to my service faithfully discharge my duty according to law.

So Help Me God

Signature of Person Enlisted L Garlepp.

Subscribed at Broadmeadows in the State of Victoria

this Sixth day of September 19 42

Before me—

Signature of Attesting Officer Kar Bradley Major

† Persons who object to take an oath may make an affirmation in accordance with the Third Schedule of the Defence Act. In such case the above form will be amended accordingly and initialed by the Attesting Officer.

D.3064/4.41.—C.4971/41

By Authority: H. E. Daw, Government Printer, Melbourne.

SERVICE AND CASUALTY FORM

A.F. B.103—1 (Adapted)

Army No. VX.100612

Unit 1 Aust. Bulk Pet. Storage Coy

Surname GARLEPP (Block Capitals)

Rank. Sgt. (On Enlistment)	Christian Names Norman Leslie

Date of Enlistment 15 August 1940

Place Footscray (?) Victoria

Date and Place of Birth 12/4/1918 Glenferrie Vic

Trade or Occupation Rubber Worker

Religion Catholic

Marital Condition Single

Next of Kin Mrs L Garlepp

Address of Next of Kin Flat 1 Bramore Buildings
255 Smith St St Kilda Frnt 93 Richmond Vic

Relationship Mother Wife

Identification—Colour of Hair Brown Eyes Brown

Distinctive Marks

Medical Classification— Class I B.2 bond
Class II 17/3/45 VSoR
(On Enlistment)

NOTHING TO BE WRITTEN IN THIS SPACE.

Record of all casualties regarding promotions (acting, temporary, local or substantive), appointments, transfers, postings, attachments, &c., forfeiture of pay, wounds, accidents, admission to and discharge from Hospital, Casualty Clearing Station, &c., Date of disembarkation and embarkation from a theatre of war (including furlough, &c.).

Report Date	From whom received	Record	Date of Casualty	Place of Casualty	Authority W.3011, B.103, or other Document	Initials of Officer Certifying Correctness of Entries
	Area 22A	Taken on Strength				
		Transferred in from 13 SPC	27.3.41	Broadmeadows Camp Rout 473/41		
		Promoted to Lance Corporal	27.5.41		Rout 135/41	
		Admitted 1 ACD Station Broadmeadows	6.6.41			
		Discharged from "	16.6.41			
		Promoted L. to Corporal	6.6.41	" "	Rout 3/41	
		Promoted Sergeant	1.8.41	" "	1101/41	
		Pvt to ollion LBP Sch Melbourne	11.9.41	" "	Rout 23/41	
		Rel to Unit	26.9.41	" "	Rout 20/41	
13.11.41	120 R.C.C.T.	Detached non Comy Luka-Larmu	35/4/41		13.11.41 "	
22.11.41	"	Re Unit from Stanley Duties	27.4.41.9		W.311.76	
8.12.41	"	Attached to CASC Aust A Echell	42.41.41.9		W.311.341	

158

VX100612 Sgt. Leslie GARLEPP

REPORT		Record of all casualties regarding promotions (acting, temporary, local or substantive), appointments, transfers, postings, attachments, &c., forfeiture of pay, wounds, accidents, admission to and discharge from Hospital, Casualty Clearing Stations, &c. Date of disembarkation and embarkation from a theatre of war (including furlough, &c.).	Date of Casualty	Place of Casualty	Authority W.3011, B.3065, or other Document	Initials of Officer Certifying Correctness of Entries
Date	From whom received					
28.12.41	120 R.M.T.		3.12.41.9		W3011 3/41	
5.6.42	"		30.12.41.9		36 Lou	
"	"					
2.6.42	115 G.H.H. Boy		31.12.41.9			
6.6.42	"				W3034 129	
12.6.42	20 R.M.T.				W3011 157	
2.6.42	Rec. Camp				N3011	
26.2.42	120 A.G.T.		14.9.42/27		117	
27.2.42	B.I.P.O.D		4.7.42/149		W3011	
3.9.42	"		4.5. 42/150		W3011 102	
27.10.42	B.I.P.O.D.		4.7.42/120		11/42	
23.1.43	"					
3.2.43	"				N3011 57	
9.2.43	"					
11.2.43	"					
20.2.43	"					

Lieut.
for Officer in Charge District Records Office
3rd M.D.

NOTHING TO BE WRITTEN IN THIS SPACE

SERVICE AND CASUALTY FORM

Continuation Sheet to A.F. B.103—1.

VX. Sgt. GARLEPP Leslie

REPORT		Record of all casualties regarding promotions (acting, temporary, local or substantive), appointments, transfers, postings, attachments, &c., forfeiture of pay, wounds, accidents, admission to and discharge from Hospital, Casualty Clearing Stations, &c. Date of disembarkation and embarkation from a theatre of war (including furlough, &c.).	Date of Casualty	Place of Casualty	Authority W.3011, B.2069, or other Document	Signature of Officer Certifying Correctness of Entries
Date	From whom received					
2-8-43	A.R.O.	Embarked "Cyprea Torika"	2-2-43	Nhdof Chua	R337/3/173)	
7-6-43	1ABSPDC	Disembarked Port Moresby N.G. ex Cypres Torika	3/11/43		W3012	
8-3-44	2/5AGH	Evac (Nbur & Eg, Tonofi) Bilateral	1-4-43	N.G.	43034	
		Post (India) †time to X Lst	4/11/44			
			12.2.44			
5.3.44	1	Disch to N.G.D.D	5/44		W3034	
10.3.44	1A B.P.S.C.	M.O.S. from N.G.D.D	14.3.44		W3011/22	
8-9-44	982 Aust Bn	Embarked at Port Moresby on Duy Stat	7-3.44		31/D/24/76	
31.8.44	1A B.B.S.C.	+ disembarked at Brisbane	31.8.44			
		Transferred 16 Aust Bulk Petroleum	4-9.44			
		Storage Coy.	9/44		W3011-22	
			31.8.44			
2/9/44	16 Aust BPS Coy	Tfd ee 1 Aust BPS Coy	28/9/44		W301	
19/11/44		Tfa P Aust 2/6 Coy BPS			M653	
19/11/44	B.1P.O.C.	Taf from 16 Aust B.O.S Coy	19/11/44		M6173	
14/12/44		Euade. such to adnn. 12 C Koch (N.Y.?)	14/12/44		W3884	
5/12/44		disch 12 C. Koch to unit (N.Y.?)	15/11/44		W3032	
23-12-44		Rel 16 d Y.D for star to Vic P. oft	19/12/43		W3011	

NOTHING TO BE WRITTEN IN THIS SPACE.

Officer I/c. Qland Egt. and Rec. Lt. Col.

SERVICE AND CASUALTY FORM

A.F. B.103—2 (Adapted)

Continuation Sheet to A.F. B.103—I.

Sgt. GARLEPP . Leslie

REPORT		Record of all casualties regarding promotions (acting, temporary, local or substantive), appointments, transfers, postings, attachments, &c., forfeiture of pay, wounds, accidents, admission to and discharge from Hospital, Casualty Clearing Stations, &c. Date of disembarkation and embarkation from a theatre of war (including furlough, &c.).	Date of Casualty	Place of Casualty	Authority W.3011, B.2069, or other Document	Signature of Officer Certifying Corrections of Entries
Date	From whom received					
20/1/45	B1 P.O.T	Reg Mbrn per casualty of attachment 16 (New Lg6 Cruo) P.T.6	15/1/45	Morotai 16	AO 3231/45	
6/2/45	B1 P.O.T	Medical Classification received at B2 (Buns N.C.)	17/1/45		AO 57/36/45	
7/3/45	B1 P.O.T	August totes. Stal to Illuos B.O.T	17/3/45		M A3R/0/131/38/45	Wells
22/3/45	3 BOD	Trans in from NSW kef csua B1 POD	14/45 V739		Wob 3	
		(Auchy LHQ SM 21500)	14/45 V739		72/45	Mills
		Trans Cud to 12:c Lefe Pres AA x6DD	19/3/45	Nchyfc		
		for Disch. Auth. MTR.R V.34457.	23/45 V.739		10/3/45	Wells
7.6.45	"		5.6.45		Roy.R. 1053	
5.6.45	C DD	MARCHED IN FOR DISCHARGE EX INT	5-6-45	Roy.R. 1053 16991		
		REALLOTMENT			07 SEP 1945	
		DISCHARGED 7/3/87			GRATUITY CHECKED	
9-6-46	C-DD	is'harged A.M.R.O.253A R 184A H.				
		Authority 16490 Date 7-6-45				
					154/45/A9337	Royal R. 136/45
			8-6-45		154/45/A9337	

NOTHING TO BE WRITTEN IN THIS SPACE.

R 23/6/45.

Lieut.
Officer i/c Records Office
Vic. L. of C. Area

161

VICTORIA L OF C AREA   Local Form A1,445

PROCEEDINGS ON DISCHARGE

PART I,   -   To be compiled by Vic. Ech. & Rec.

1. Army No. *VX 100612* Rank *SGT* Unit *1st Bulk Petroleum Storage*

   N a m e   *GARLEPP   LESLIE*
   (In full, Surname in BLOCK letters)

   Vic. L of C Auth: *16690* Date: *7 JUN 1945*   AMR&O 253A(1)   *H*

   REASON FOR DISCHARGE: (in words) *Tread Extruder*
   Operator   (Rubber Industry)

2. TRADE GROUP in which employed at time of DISCHARGE: _____

3. MARITAL CONDITION: *SINGLE*   DATE OF BIRTH: *12/7/1918*

                              COMPUTED AS AT: *7 JUN 1945*

4. PERIOD OF SERVICE: (Showing CMF, AIF, etc separately)

	Total Eff. Service
(a) Enlisted for the *CMF* on *17.3.41* and who served on CONTINUOUS FULL TIME WAR SERVICE: with:--	*1544 1546* days. (which includes)
the *CMF* from *17-3-41* to *6.9.42*	A/S IN Australia *598 599* days.
and *A-I-F* from *6.9.42* to _____	A/S o/s Australia.
and _____ from _____ to _____	*553 553* days.

   (b) NON EFFECTIVE SERVICE: (Consecutive periods of 21 days or over for which member NOT entitled to receive pay, to be shown ONLY)

A.W.L. NOT involving Detention		DAYS	DETENTION etc. including automatic forfeitures		DAYS	LEAVE WITHOUT PAY		DAYS
FROM	TO		FROM	TO		FROM	TO	

5. SERVICE QUALIFYING WAR BADGE:

	Overseas Destination	Embarked FROM Aust.	Disembarked IN Australia.	DAYS	Northern Territory and/or Torres Strait Islands.
(a)	*N.G*	*2/3/43*	*4/9/44*	*553*	Stationed At _____
(b)		/ /	/ /		from / /
(c)		/ /	/ /		to / /

6. DECORATIONS & AWARDS: _____

7. DISABILITY: _____

   _____

   MED. CLASSIFICATION: *B2*   Degree of Disability: _____

"x"   COMPILED BY: *Emma Sgt VX 92073*   Pers. Records Sect.
"x"   COMPUTATIONS BY: *V12068 W/Sgt Roy Nichols*   Disch. & R/S Sect.
"x"   CHECKED BY: *VX 10161*   Disch. & R/S Sect.
"x"   FINAL COMPUTATIONS: *VX 549*   Vic. Ech. & Rec. Det.
"x"   (State Army Number Rank & Name)   G.D.D.

After Leslie left the army, he married Lillian May McCrory (1919–2016) when he was 24 and she was 22. Lillian was the daughter of John McRory (1888–1980) and Sylvia Gladys (nee Oliver 1895–1953).

Here is a copy of an invitation to their wedding.

Mr. & Mrs. J. McCRORY
Request the pleasure of the Company of

Mr & Mrs. P. Oliver

At the Marriage of their Daughter,

MAY
To

SGT. LESLIE GARLIPP
At

The Methodist Church, Fitzroy Street, St. Kilda,

on

Saturday, April 25, 1942, At 4.30 p.m.

BREAKFAST at Rainbow Hall, 138 Commercial Road, Prahran, at 6 p.m. sharp.

25 Smith Street, St. Kilda.

R.S.V.P. Before April 10, 1942.

Leslie and Lillian lived at 389 Punt Road, Richmond in 1942 where Leslie was working as a Rubber worker.

In 1968 they were living at 73 Tumut Street, Adelong, New South Wales, where Leslie was employed as a process worker.

On 7 March, 1987 Leslie died at 89 Lynch Street Adelong New South Wales. He was 68 years of age.

Lillian died 20 August, 2016 in Queensland at the age of 97.

Charles Henry Garlepp	1884–1949
married	
Clara Maud Harnden	1888-1982
children	
John Joseph Garlepp	1909–2000
married	1933
Eve Christina Stubbs	1908–1989
children	
Jocelyn Garlepp	1934–
married	
Harry Thomas Godden	
John Barry Garlepp	1937–2010
married	
Barbara	
children	
Lucas Garlepp	
Andrea Garlepp	
Fiona Garlepp	
Adam Garlepp	
Diane Garlepp	1947–
Michael Charles Garlepp	1951–2020
Patricia	
children	
Nicholas	
Joanna	
Ivy Agnes Garlepp	1910–
married	1943
Leslie Richard Burton	1917–1995
married or partner	around 1954
Lindsay William Deppeler	1919–1980
Ernest Edward Garlepp	1912–1914
Charles Henry Garlepp	1912–1913
William Patrick Garlepp	about 1915-
married	1938
Minnie Elsie Hansen	1915–2004
Leslie Michael Garlepp	1918–1987
married	1938
Lillian May McCrory	1919-2016

Ernest Edward Garlepp was born 28 March, 1886 in Baddaginnie Victoria. He was the second child of Ernest (1866-1936) and Ellen Garlepp (nee French 1866-1931).

When Ernest was 22 , he married Ethel May Robertson (1886-1954) . Ethel was born 8 September, 1885 in South Melbourne, Victoria. Ethel was the daughter of William Falconer Robertson (1852–1905) and Catherine Forbes (1852–1899).

Ernest and Ethel had the following children:

Ethel May Garlepp	1909–1997
Veronica Mavis Garlepp	1912–1933
Lillian Irene Garlepp	1915–1974
Dorothy May Garlepp	1921–1978

In 1914 the family were living at 9 Milton Place, South Richmond and Ernest was working as a labourer.

Below is photo of Ernest Edward and Ethel May taken around 1911.

GOT HIS BEER, BUT MADE IT EXPENSIVE

A man apparently under the influence of intoxicating liquor carrying a kitbag "bristling" with bottled beer tried to pass through an inlet barrier at Flinders Street station just after 4 p.m. yesterday, Cecil Henry Homes, a special railway ticket checker, said in the City Court today in evidence of a disturbance with two men.

Constable Leo O'Dwyer told the court that William Edward Brennan, 37, of Station Street, Edithvale, was carrying eight bottles of beer The bottles, he said, were poking out of the top of the bag in all directions.

For having behaved offensively and used insulting words near the Flinders Street barriers, Brennan was fined £5 in default 21 days' imprisonment.

Wilfred Davis Graham, 41, of Green Street, Windsor, who, according to evidence, interfered when Brennan was told he could not take the beer on the train, was fined £3 on an insulting words charge, in default 14 days' imprisonment.

In 1926 when she was just 16, Ethel May married William Edward Brennan (1906-1956) They had four children, two of them were:

Keith John Brennan	1930–2023
William George Brennan	1931–1984

Ethel loved and bred British Bulldogs. I found the article above in the Herald on 22 December, 1943.

William died in 1956.

By 1928 the family were living 18 Gilbert Road, Ivanhoe.

On 30 April, 1933, their daughter Veronica died. She was just 21 years old and there was an inquest.

If you would like to look at the Inquest report you will find it Public Record Office Victoria Collection | PROV

According to the 30 April, 1933 police report, "Veronica was admitted to the Women's Hospital, Carlton, suffering from the effects of a threatened abortion. She was attended to by Doctor Howard, although abortion did not take place, Miss Garlepp became progressively worse and died at about 5.10 pm from uraemia.

Deceased was a single woman and resided with her parents and sister at 18 Gilbert Road, Ivanhoe. She had been unemployed for the past three months, prior to that she had been employed in a fancy leather goods factory in Clifton Hill.

On the 26th instant and again on the 27th instant with Detective I interviewed deceased at the Women's Hospital, Carlton. She informed us that she was two months pregnant; that she had been taking medicine twice daily prior to being admitted to the hospital, for the purpose of bringing about an abortion; that the medicine had been given to her by another person; and that she had taken the whole of the medicine and had discarded the bottle.

On further questioning deceased refused to give us any information regarding the person who gave her the medicine, or who was responsible for her condition.

Later deceased told her mother where the bottle was from which she had taken the medicine and that the bottle still contained a small portion of the medicine."

When the bottle of medicine was examined it was found to be an extract of ergot.

Ethel, Veronica's mother said when she was deposed: "Deceased, Veronica Mavis Garlepp, was my daughter. She was 21 years old and resided with me at 18 Gilbert Road, Ivanhoe. About the 6th of April I noticed that deceased did not come unwell and I spoke to her about it, but she denied that there was anything wrong with her. About the 14th of April, 1933 I noticed that deceased had her clothes packed up,

I said to her, "Is there anything wrong with you?" She said "Yes" I did not ask deceased how long she had been pregnant. I frequently asked deceased who was responsible for her condition, but she would say "It is no one in Ivanhoe." On the 20th of April, 1933, about midday deceased fell in the doorway of the lavatory, I said to her, "You are sick". Deceased said, "I will be alright in a little while." I put deceased to bed and sent for Dr Hayes. I heard deceased tell Dr Hayes that she went somewhere. Dr Hayes said "Was it a doctor?". Deceased said "Yes" Dr Hayes said "What doctor?" Deceased said "I can't tell you that, or words to that effect. Dr Hayes gave me a letter and I conveyed deceased to the Women's Hospital, at Carlton, the same day. I visited deceased daily at the women's Hospital. On the 29th of April, 1933 deceased said to me "There is some medicine at home which I have been taking, will you bring it in to me, I promised it to the doctor." I said Where is it?

She said "In the pantry amongst the jam jars." I searched amongst the jars in the pantry at my home and found the bottle of medicine produced. On the 30th of April, 1933 I took this medicine to the hospital and I handed it to a doctor. I did not ask deceased where she got the medicine. To my knowledge deceased did not keep company with any boy. Deceased very seldom went out at night. She did not tell me how long she had been pregnant. "

The Inquest found Veronica had died from Toxic nephritis due to lead poisoning and septic abortion procured by herself the said deceased.

This notice was placed in The Age on 2 May 1933

GARLEPP.—On the 30th April, at Women's Hospital, Veronica Mavis, dearly beloved daughter of Ernest and Ethel Garlepp, of 18 Gilbert-road, Ivanhoe, and loving sister of Ethel (Mrs. Brennan), Lily and Dorothy, aged 21 years. R.I.P.

In 1936 the family moved to 30 Stanley Street, Richmond South.

Dorothy married John Lewis Kennaugh (1914-) in 1939. Lillian never married and remained living with her parents.

Ernest died at age 62, on 16 August 1948. He was buried at the Fawkner Cemetery.

After Ernest died, Ethel found work as a process worker and moved to 109 Mary Street, Richmond.

Ethel died in 24 November, 1954 and was buried with Ernest at Fawkner Cemetery.

The notice to the right was found in The Argus 17 august, 1948.

The notice below right was found in The Age 25 November, 1954.

Barry, loved grandson of Mrs. W. E. Barry, of South Yarra.
GARLEPP. — On August 16, Ernest, dearly beloved husband of Ethel May, and beloved father of Ethel (Mrs. Brennan), Dorothy (Mrs. Kennaugh), Lily, and Veronica (deceased). —Requiescat in pace.

GARLEPP.—On November 24 (suddenly), Ethel May, beloved wife of the late Ernest and loving mother of Ethel Veronica (deceased), Lillian and Dorothy; grandmother of Pat, Joan, Bill, Keith, Barry and Yvonne.

167

This photo is about 1912. Ernest Edward is sitting with probably Lillian on his lap. Ethel is in the doorway with Ethel in front of her. I would love to know what property they are at, and who the other woman, man and boy are.

Mary Ann Garlepp was the third child of Ernest (1866-1936) and Ellen Garlepp (nee French 1866-1931). She was born in Yarrawonga, Victoria in 1889.

In 1908 Mary married Richard Barton (1888-1913). In 1904 Richard had married Edith Duff and in the Police Gazette on 10 July, 1908 there was a warrant for him. It gives a great description of what he looked like.

RICHARD BARTON is charged, on warrant, with disobeying an order of the Hawthorn Bench to find a surety of £25, and to pay 15s. per week for the maintenance of his wife. Description :—A labourer, 20 years of age, 5 feet 5 inches high, thin build, small fair moustache, dark hair, cast in left eye, scar on right side of forehead and lower lip; wore a blue serge sac coat, tweed trousers and vest, black boxer hat or light tweed cap, and black button-up boots. —O.4252A. 10th July, 1908.

I cannot find any divorce from Edith, nor can I find any records about what the outcome was of the warrant.

Mary and Richard were to have 3 children, the first two unfortunately died in infancy.

Lilly Agnes Barton	1908–1908
Charles William Barton	1909–1910
Kathleen Barton	1910–1979

On 28 December, 1913, Richard died in the Melbourne Hospital, he was only 25. He was interred at the Springvale Necropolis.

In 1915 Mary Ellen married Charles Arthur May (1878-1939). They farmed in Pakenham for the rest of their lives. They had at least two more children

Charles Clement May	1916-1976
Dorothy Helen	?-1983

Kathleen Barton (Katie) married James Bertie Dunn (1906-1979) in 1929. They lived in the Pakenham area. They had the following children:

Leonard James Charles Dunn	1929–2016
David George Dunn	1936–2001
Graham Godfrey Dunn	1938–1984
Lilian Myrtle Dunn	1945–2007
Colin Dunn	
Kathleen Dunn	
Albert Dunn	

Charles Clement May fought in New Guinea during the second world war. He was a farmer in Pakenham.

And Dorothy Helen May married Frederick Lewis. .

Ethel Maude was the fourth child of Ernest (1864-1936) and Ellen Garlepp (1866-1931) she was born 17 June 1891 in Port Melbourne, Victoria.

In 1909, Ethel had a son, who's father was 'unknown' on his birth registration. He was born in Hawthorn, Victoria.

William Henry Garlepp   1909-1941

Ethel married Daniel James Tierney (1885-1957) in 1914. Daniel was the son of Patrick and Mary (nee Nelson). He was born in Box Hill, Victoria.

They had 2 children:

Nellie Irene Tierney   1915-1915
Lorna May Tierney   1916-1995

The family lived at 1 Oswin Street, Kew and Daniel worked as a labourer.

mother of Rhonda (Mrs. Bell).
TIERNEY.—On May 1. at her residence. 1 Oswin Street. East Kew,
Ethel Maude. dearly loved wife of
Daniel James Tierney, loving mother
of William (deceased), Nellie (deceased) and Lorna (Mrs. J. Keillor), fond mother-in-law of Jean
and Jonn, loving gran of Jim,
Patricia, Jack, Shirley and Tom
Tierney, and Fay and Anthony Keillor. Privately interred
             Requiescat in pace.

Ethel died 1 May, 1953. Here is a death notice for her found in The Age on 5 May, 1953.

Daniel died in May, 1957 and was buried in the Box Hill Cemetery.

William took on his step fathers name of Tierney. He married Jean Irene McLean (1909-1998) on 28 August, 1932. William and Jean lived at 60 First Avenue, Kew in 1936 and William was working a labourer. The couple had 5 children:

Shirley Tierney
Jack Tierney
Pat Tierney
James Tierney
Tom Tierney

William died on 18 July, 1941 after being struck by a car in Melbourne. This article was in the Age on 19 July, 1941.

Injured

Two men were injured, one fatally. when they were struck by a motor car at the corner of Flinders and Spencer streets, city, yesterday. William Tierney, 31 years, First-avenue, Kew, received a fracture of the skull, and died in Royal Melbourne Hospital several hours after admission. Clarence Armstrong, 47 years, Power-street, Hawthorn, received a possible fracture of the skull and fractured ribs. He is in Royal Melbourne Hospital.

TIERNEY.—On May 1, at her residence. 1 Oswin Street. East Kew,
Ethel Maude. dearly loved wife of
Daniel James Tierney, loving mother
of William (deceased), Nellie (deceased) and Lorna (Mrs. J. Keillor), fond mother-in-law of Jean
and Jonn, loving gran of Jim,
Patricia, Jack, Shirley and Tom
Tierney, and Fay and Anthony Keillor. Privately interred
             Requiescat in pace.

This death notice was in the Age on 5 May, 1953.

Lorna married John Keillor (1903-1967) on 25June, 1935 in Kew. The couple had at least 2 children:

Faye Lorraine Keillor   1936–2013
Anthony Keillor

John died 11 February, 1967 and Lorna died 12 September, 1995. They are buried in the Templestowe cemetery.

——-

John Joseph (Jack) Garlepp was born 5 December, 1894 in Port Melbourne, Victoria. He was the fifth child of Ernest (1864-1936) and Ellen Garlepp (1866-1931). He is my Great Grand Father.

When he was still a baby the family were living in Heathcote, Victoria and around 1898 they were living in Montrose Street, Hawthorn. In 1902 they had moved to 40 Brunswick Road, Brunswick and in 1906 they were living at 196 Barkers Road, Hawthorn, where his father is a Railway Worker.

In 1917 Jack married Daisy McFadden, my great grandmother. Daisy McFadden was born in 1895 in Steiglitz, Victoria. Daisy was the tenth child of James McFadden (1856-1923) and Catherine Jane Graham (1856-1939).

The couple were living at 131 Cubitt Street, Cremorne in 1919 and Jack was working as a labourer.

Jack and Daisy had 2 children:

Gloria 'Betty' Mena Garlepp   1918–2015

Lorna Garlepp   1920–2012

/ The Age (Melbourne, Vic. : 1854 - 1954) / Sat 5 Nov 1921

FREEMAN.—On the 3rd November, at her son's residence, 20 Hartman-street, Kensington, Louisa Freeman, late of Grant-street, Ballarat East, aged 74. At rest.

GARLEPP.—On the 22nd October, at St. Vincent's Hospital, after a short illness, John Joseph, beloved husband of Daisy and loving daddy of Mena and Lorna, beloved youngest son of Ernest and Ellen Garlepp, of Yatpool, loving brother of Charlie (Ivanhoe), Ernest (Richmond), Ethel (Mrs. Tierney, Glenferrie), Katie (Mrs. Beale, Carwarp), Mary (Mrs. May, Pakenham) and Lily (Mrs. Matthews, Yatpool, deceased), aged 26 years.

O sacred heart of Jesus, have mercy on his poor soul. —Inserted by C. and M. May, Pakenham.

On 21 October, 1921, after a short illness, Jack died in the St Vincent's Hospital. He was 26 years old. He was buried in the Box Hill Cemetery.

This death notice was in the Age on 5 November, 1921.

Daisy remarried in 1926 to George Edward McCann (1900-1989) and gave birth to another daughter on 7 November, 1923, Norma Louisa Daisy McCann (1928-1995).

In 1949 Daisy and George were living at 23 Railway Place, Williamstown and George was working as a mechanic.   A picture of the house is below. On 30 May, 1952 there was two articles about the landlord who tried to evict Daisy and George. The first was in The Williamstown Chronicle and the second was in Williamstown Advertiser.

* WAR PENSIONER'S HOUSING WORRY

Pensioner in respect of two world wars, John Day, of Giffard St., Williamstown, sought an eviction order in Williamstown Court on Tuesday last against George Edward Mc-Cann, fisherman, and Mrs. Mc-Cann, in relation to a house owned by applicant in Railway Place, Williamstown.

Applicant said he had owned the subject premises for three years. Defendants were the tenants, and had been served with a notice to quit. A ward was living with applicant and his wife in a house in Giffard Street for which 25/- was being paid as rent. Applicant was receiving 25/- a week from the house he owned in Railway Place and out of this he had to pay rates, taxes and com-

mission. He alleged his property had been damaged by defendant.

Defendant.—Will you admit the place is in a very bad condition?

Applicant.—Yes.

Defendant stated the damage was due to fair wear and tear. In his family was his wife, a son aged 18, a grandson aged 15, a daughter and son-in law and their two children. Defendant had made efforts to get another home, but the position was hopeless.

The case was adjourned for three months, and defendant was asked by Mr. Hammond, SM, to make intensive efforts in the meantime to find other accommodation.

Old Soldier Wants His House

An ex-serviceman pensioner, who saw service in two world wars, John Day, of 34 Giffard Street, sought possession of a house which he purchased at 23 Railway Place, in an application to the local court on Tuesday for an eviction order against his tenants, Mr. and Mrs. McCann.

Day, who was represented by Mr. T. Kennedy, claimed that the house was reasonably required for his wife and himself, and alleged that the tenants were responsible for about half-a-dozen weatherboards being missing from outside the kitchen wall, and a lavatory pan being broken.

The applicant said that a young ward was also living with his wife and himself and that he had recently been an inmate of the Heidelberg Hospital for twelve months. He added that the owner of the house in which he is now living desired possession.

In cross-examination, the tenant, George Edward McCann, asked: Will you admit that the place is in a very bad condition?

Day: Yes, I will admit that.

McCann testified that the house was in such a condition that the weatherboards fell off, they would not hold the nails. He had not been responsible for removing any weatherboards. Living with his wife and himself in the house were his daughter, son-in-law and two grandchildren.

Questioned by Mr. Kennedy, he said that he had made efforts to get another home but it was hopeless.

The magistrate. Mr. Hammond, decided to adjourn the case until August 26, and said that in the meantime the tenants must make extensive enquiries into the possibility of getting another house.

Daisy died on 10 November, 1978 and was buried in the Altona Cemetery. George died 12 January, 1989.

Gloria Mena Garlepp, Daisy's eldest daughter was my Grandmother, she married Leslie Tunes (1915-1978) on 14 October, 1935.

Leslie was born, in Maryborough, as Leslie Brogan on 30 June 1915 to Lillian Myrtle Cornwill (1893-1935) and Henry Brogan (1886-1974) although the Birth Certificate has Lillian Myrtle Brogan and unknown father.   The Victorian Births Deaths and Marriage registry tracked down this information for us many years age. To make matters more confusing, from early childhood, Leslie lived with his grandmother, Emma Harris (1867-1943) and her defacto husband, Alfred George Tunes (1868-1939) and took the surname of Tunes.

Sometimes Leslie used the name Peter Simpson, we don't know why. He may have got the name Simpson from his mothers second husband , Ernest Simpson who she married when Leslie was about 2 years of age.

Mena and Leslie had 4 children:

Leslie John Tunes	1936–2016
married	1954
Barbara Louise Vine	1935-1993
children	
Debra Louise Tunes	1954-
Robyn Lesleigh Tunes	1956-
Kerri-Ann Elizabeth Tunes	1958-
Peter Albert Maxwell Leslie	1961-
Partner	
Patricia Phillis Parsisson	1941-
children	
Collindy Suzanne Parsisson	1963-
Leslie John Parsisson	1966-
Lillian Merle Tunes	1937–
married	1956
William Roger Richards	
Donald Lawrence Tunes	1939–
married	
Gael Smith	
Janice Marlene Tunes	1940–
married	1960
Harry Ernest Pengelly	
children	
Andrew Pengelly	
Kim Pengelly	
Deanne Pengelly	

Mena and Leslie divorced and Mena remarried in 1955 to Maxwell James Pinnell (1921-2000)

In 1958 Mena and Maxwell were living at 14 Zinnia Street Reservoir and Max was a driver.

Max died 20 July, 2000 and Mena died 8 July 1915 at the age of 97.

——-

Lorna Merle Garlepp was born in Richmond, Victoria, on 26 October, 1920 and was the second child of John Joseph Garlepp (1894-1921) and Daisy (nee McFadden 1895–1978). In 1949 Lorna married Henry Carrum Jones (1898–1985). Henry was the son of John James Jones (1856–1942) and Elizabeth Ann (nee Goodall 1868–1944). He was born in Melbourne, Victoria.

When Henry was 19 he enlisted in the Army. He fought in France. His records show that he had been wounded and had been gassed. It would have been awful. He was returned to Australia 20 November 1918.

When he returned he lived in family home until he married Lorna in 1949. Henry was a stair case builder.

Lorna and Henry had at least one child:

Janette Elizabeth Jones   1952–2006

The family lived at 27 Clive Road, Auburn for many years. I have a picture on the following page.

Around 1970 Henry and Lorna moved to a unit at 1/372 Abbotsford Street, North Melbourne.

Henry died 26 September, 1985 and was buried in the Box Hill Cemetery.

Lorna died 19 July 2012 at the age of 91 and was buried in the Box Hill Cemetery.

27 Clive Road

Auburn, Victoria

Norma Louisa Daisy McCann was Daisy McCann (nee Garlepp 1895-1978) and George Edward McCann (1900-1989). Norma was born 7 November, 1928 in Melbourne Victoria.

In 1946 when Norma was 18 years old, she married John Ambrose MacMillan (1920-1970).

Norma later partnered with Lionel Harold Prider (1917-1979). Lionel died in 1979 and Norma died 12 September, 1997 at age 67. She is buried with Lionel in the Altona Cemetery.

Katie Garlepp was born 25 May, 1899 in Hawthorn Victoria. Katie was the 6th child of Ernest (1864-1936) and Ellen French (nee French 1866–1931).

When Katie was 21, she married on 7 October, 1920 in Mildura, Richard John Beale (1892-1976). On their marriage registration Richard called himself William. Richard was the son of Andrew William Beale (1854-1932) and Christine Hannah Hyett (1856-1940). This was Richard's second marriage. When he was 19 he married Elsie Jane Hamill (1891-1964). They had a child, William Thomas Beale (1911-). Just prior to William being born, Richard and Elsie were living with his parents in Glenlyon, Victoria. Richard deserted Elsie and she finally divorced him in 1916. Below are the notices in the Victorian Police Gazette.

RICHARD JOHN BEALE is charged, on warrant, with deserting his wife, Elsie Jane Beale, Raglan-street, Daylesford, at Glenlyon, on the 13th inst. Description :—A miner, 22 years of age, 5 feet 6 or 7 inches high, thin build, dark hair, clean shaven, pale complexion, blue eyes; wore a dark-green sac suit, maroon sweater, black boxer hat; third finger nail on right hand injured.—O.3730A. 15th June, 1911.

1911

See *Police Gazette*, 1911, p. 323.

RICHARD JOHN BEALE, on warrant, for wife desertion, is believed to be in the Central District, as he recently visited his parents at Glenlyon on a bicycle.—O.3730A. 17th September, 1912.

1912

See *Police Gazette*, 1911, p. 323.

BEALE, RICHARD JOHN, on warrant, for wife desertion.— The complainant obtained a decree *nisi* at the Divorce Court, Melbourne, on the 15th inst.—O.3730A. 17th August, 1916.

1916

This article was in The Herald

15 August, 1916

WARRANT NOT EXECUTED

Elsie Jane Beale, 25, of Vincent street, Daylesford, was granted a decree nisi for divorce from Richard John Beale, 25, miner, on the ground of desertion. The parties were married on April 7, 1911, at Daylesford. There is one child. Mr R. W. Shallard, instructed by Mr J. M. Finlayson, appeared for the petitioner.

Mrs Beale gave evidence that after marriage she and her husband lived at the house of her husband's father, at Glenlyon, near Daylesford. Her husband gave her very little money, and in June, 1911, she asked him to give her a pound. He promised to do so on the following day, but instead disappeared. She had never seen him since, and a warrant issued for his arrest had not been served.

Richard, or as he was now called, William was a miner when he and Katie married. They were living in Mildura and they had a daughter in 1921

Patricia Ivy Beale   1921-

In 1931 the family had moved to Berwick and they later moved to 36 Princes Avenue, Springvale. William was working for the Railway.

There were at least 4 more children born:

Joan Beale   1927–1984
John Beale
Jessie Beale   1934–2020
Frances Audrey Beale

Katie died 23 September, 1944 at the age of 45 and was buried in the Springvale Cemetery. The following obituary was found in the Dandenong Journal 27 September, 1944.

MRS W. BEALE

Following heart trouble, which had kept her in poor health for some months, Mrs. Katie Beale, 45, wife of Mr. William Beale, of 36 Prince's avenue, Spring Vale, passed away peacefully at her home on September 23. The sympathy of the whole district goes out to her bereaved husband and family of 4 daughters and 1 son. A splendid woman in every respect, the late Mrs. Beale was a very staunch worker for St. Joseph's Church, Spring Vale, and when the funeral took place on Monday, children from St. Joseph's formed a sorrowing guard of honor as the cortege left for the Spring Vale Necropolis. Deceased's popularity was reflected in the large number of friends who offered up Mass for the repose of her soul, Rev. Fr. Keane being the celebrant, both before the altar and at the graveside. The casket was borne by Messrs. G. Luxford, L. Hiven, W. James, L. Charman, T. Brick and H. Bell, all railway workmates of the sorrowing husband and a large number of mourners attended to pay their last respects. Funeral arrangements were in the hands of W. J. Garnar and Son.

William died in 8 June, 1976 in Ararat.

He was buried in the Landsborough Cemetery.

According to the his headstone, he was a Sergaent in the 2nd Field Amb. Anzac Cor.

I have searched all the records and I cannot find any trace of military service.

The article below was in the Dandenong Journal 23 June 1954. It's about Jessie, the youngest daughter of Katie and William, and their wedding. I have transcribed it for easy reading.

Spring Vale bride, Dande. groom

A RECENT wedding of interest to Spring Vale residents was that of Jessie Maureen Beale, youngest daughter of Mr. W. Beale, 52 Princes Av., Spring Vale, to Mr. Alan Henry Peters of Dandenong.

The ceremony took place at St. Joseph's Church, Spring Vale, on Saturday, May 22nd, at 10 o'clock, and was performed by the Rev. Fr. P. A. Dougan.

The bride entered the church on her father's arm, wearing a gown of white cobweb lace over satin with long sleeves and a graceful train. Her bouquet contained carnations, roses and hyacinths and she also carried a prayer book. A long hand-embroidered veil was attached to a juliet cap.

The two bridesmaids, Irene Peters, sister of the groom, and Lorraine Anderson, friend of the bride, were frocked alike in mauve net over taffeta, trimmed with silver cornelli work. Their juliet caps matched their dresses, and they carried Victorian posies of frangipanni and violets. The bride's niece Judith Smith, made a charming flowergirl, dressed as a replica of the bridesmaids.

The groom, who is the second son of Mr. and Mrs. A. L. Peters, of Hammond Rd., Dandenong, had the bride's brother, John, for best man, while his own brother, Ron, carried out the duties of groomsman.

At a reception at the Mechanic's Hall, Spring Vale, guests were greeted by Mr. Beale and his daughter, Mrs. Smith, assisted by Mr. and Mrs. Peters.

A grey fitted coat, worn over a lemon silk shantung frock, formed the bride's travelling outfit, with which she wore black accessories and a lemon hat.

The three tiered wedding cake was made and artistically decorated by the groom's father, Mr. L. Peters.

The present address of the newlyweds is 52 Princes Av., Spring Vale.

Spring Vale bride, Dande. groom

A recent wedding of interest to Spring Vale residents was that of Jessie Maureen Beale, youngest daughter of Mr W. Beale 52 Princes Av., Spring Vale to Mr. Alan Henry Peters of Dandenong.

The ceremony took place at St Joseph's Church, Spring Vale, on Saturday May 22nd at 10 o'clock and was performed by the Rev. Fr. P. A. Dougan.

The bride entered the church on her father's arm, wearing a gown of white cobweb lace over satin with long sleeves and a graceful train. Her bouquet contained carnations, roses and hyacinths and she also carried a prayer book. A long hand embroidered veil was attached to a juliet cap.

The two bridesmaids, Irene Peters sister of the groom and Lorraine Anderson, friend of the bride, were frocked alike in a mauve net over taffeta, trimmed with silver connelli work. Their juliet caps matched their dresses, and they carried Victorian posies of frangipanni and violets. The bride's niece Judith Smith made a charming flowergirl dressed as a replica of the bridesmaids.

The groom who is the second son of Mr and Mrs A. L. Peters of Hammond Road, Dandenong, had the bride's brother John, for best man, while his own brother Ron, carried out the duties of groomsman.

At a reception at the Mechanic's Hall, Spring Vale, guests were greeted by Mr Beale and his daughter, Mrs Smith assisted by Mr and Mrs Peters.

A grey fitted coat worn over a lemon silk shantung frock formed the bride's travelling outfit, with which she wore black accessories and a lemon hat.

The three tiered wedding cake was made and artistically decorated by the groom's father Mr L Peters.

The present address of the newlyweds is 52 Princes Ave. Spring Vale.

Lilly Agnes Garlepp was born 1902–1921 was the youngest daughter of Ernest (1864-1936) and Ellen Garlepp (nee French 1866-1931). When Lilly was 18, she married Roy William Matthews (1900-1979). Roy was born 22 December, 1894 in Sydney, New South Wales. His parents were William John Matthews (1871–1941) and Minnie Alice Matthews (nee Morris 1870–1946)

On 4 December, 1920 Nellie Irene Mathews was born. Here is a copy of her Birth registration.

Unfortunately, Lilly died 16 August, 1921 when Nellie was just a few months old.

Ernest and Ellen placed the following memorial in The Age on 17 August, 1925.

MATHEWS (nee Garlepp).—In sad and loving memory of our dear daughter, Lilly Agnes, who passed away at Mildura on 16th August, 1921, loving mother of little Nell.   R.I.P.
        To-day brings back sad memories
        Of our dear ones gone to rest.
    And those who think of her to-day
        Are those who loved her best.
    Immaculate heart of Mary,
        Your prayers for her extol;
    O, sacred heart of Jesus,
        Have mercy on her soul.
—Inserted by her loving parents, Ernest and Ellen Garlepp, Bittern.

Roy went on to marry again in 1927 to Elsie Annie McPhail (1895–1960). They had the following children which would be half siblings to Nellie Irene.

Letitia Marie Matthews	1923–2011
Kevin Morris Matthews	1928–2002
Ailya Jean Matthews	1930–2016
Beth Elsie Matthews	1937–2006

Roy served in the second world war and where he attained the rank of Lance Corporal. Roy died 30 January, 1972

Ernest Garlepp 1864-1936 descendants were:

married	1884
Ellen French	1866–1931
Children	
Charles Henry Garlepp	1884–1949
married	1907
Clara Maud Harnden	1888–1982
children	
John Joseph Garlepp	1909–2000
married	1933
Eve Christina Stubbs	1908–1989
children	
Jocelyn Garlepp	1934–
John Barry Garlepp	1937–2010
Diane Garlepp	1947–
Michael Charles Garlepp	1951–2020
Patricia Garlepp	
Ivy Agnes Garlepp	1911–1980
married	1943
Leslie Richard Burton	1917–1995
Partner	
Lindsay William Deppeler	1919–1980
Ernest Edward Garlepp	1912–1914
Charles Henry Garlepp	1912–1913
William Patrick Garlepp	1915–
married	1938
Minnie Elsie Hansen	1913–2004
Leslie Michael Garlepp	1918–1987
married	1942
Lillian May McCrory	1919–2016
Ernest Edward Garlepp	1886–1948
married	1908
Ethel May Robertson	1885–1954
children	
Ethel May Garlepp	1909–1997
married	1926
William Edward (Ted) Brennan	1906–1956
children	
Keith John Brennan	1930–2023
William George Brennan	1931–1984
Pat Brennan	

Veronica Mavis Garlepp	1912–1933
Lillian Irene Garlepp	1915–1974
Dorothy May Garlepp	1921–1977
married	1939
John Lewis Kennaugh	1914–
children	
Barry john Kennaugh	
Mary Ellen Garlepp	1889–1941
married	1908
Richard Barton	1888–1913
children	
Lilly Agnes Barton	1908–1908
Charles William Barton	1909–1910
Kathleen Barton	1910–1979
married	1915
Charles Arthur May	1878–1939
children	
Charles Clement May	1916–1976
Dorothy Helen May	–1982
Ethel Maud Garlepp	1891–1953
children	
William Henry Garlepp	1909–1941
married	1932
Jean Irene McLean	1909–1998
children	
Tom Tierney	
Shirley Tierney	
Jack Tierney	
Pat Tierney	
James Tierney	
married	1914
Daniel Jas Tierney	1885–1957
children	
Nellie Irene Tierney	1915–1915
Lorna May Tierney	1916–1995
married	1935
John Keillor	1903–1967
children	
Faye Lorraine Keillor	1936–2013
Anthony Keillor	

John Joseph (Jack) Garlepp	1894–1921
married	1917
Daisy McFadden	1895–1978
children	
Gloria Mena Garlepp	1918–2015
married	1935
Leslie (Peter Tunes) Brogan	1915–1978
children	
Leslie John Tunes	1936–2016
Lillian Merle Tunes	1937–
Donald Lawrence Tunes	1939–
Janice Marlene Tunes	1940–
married	1955
Maxwell James Pinnell	1921–2000
Lorna Merle Garlepp	1920–2012
married	1949
Henry Carrum Jones	1898–1985
children	
Janette Elizabeth Jones	1952–2006
married	1926
George Edward McCann	1900–1989
children	
Norma Louisa Daisy McCann	1928–1995
married	1946
John Ambrose MacMillan	1920–1970
Partner	
Lionel Harold Prider	1917–1979
Katie Garlepp	1899–1944
married	1924
Richard John Beale	1892–1976
children	
Patricia Ivy Beale	1921–
Joan Beale	1927–1984
John Beale	ab1930–
Jessie Beale	1934–2020
Frances Audrey Beale	
Lily Agnes Garlepp	1902–1921
married	1920
Roy William Matthews	1894–1972
children	
Nellie Irene Matthews	1920–2014

Index

Colleen Maree Garlepp	1956–2013	john Garlepp	1851–1851
Coral Lorraine Garlepp		John Garlepp	1853–1912
Deborah Garlepp		John Garlepp	
Diane Garlepp	1947–	John Jonas GARLEPP	1891–1922
Dorothy May Garlepp	1921–1977	John Joseph (Jack) Garlepp	1894–1921
Edith May GARLEPP	1914–1914	John Joseph GARLEPP	1909–2000
Edward Garlepp	1901–1931	John Joseph Garlepp	1927–1957
Edward Patrick Garlepp	1917–1974	John Patrick Garlepp	1920–1984
Elizabeth Anistasia Garlepp	1886–1886	John Patrick Garlepp	1928–1955
Elizabeth Cornelia Brauer/Brown	1821–	Kathleen Alma Garlepp	1922–2013
Ellen Garlepp	1887–1942	Kathleen GARLEPP	1889–1956
Emma Elizabeth Garlepp	1879–1904	Kathleen Mary Garlepp	1920–1980
Ernest Edward Garlepp	1886–1948	Katie GARLEPP	1899–1944
Ernest Edward Garlepp	1891–1971	Leslie Michael Garlepp	1918–1987
Ernest Edward Garlepp	1912–1914	Lillian Irene Garlepp	1915–1974
Ernest Garlepp	1864–1936	Lillian May Garlepp	1924–1995
Ernest John Garlepp	1909–1993	Lily Agnes Garlepp	1902–1921
Ethel Maud Garlepp	1891–1953	Lorna Merle Garlepp	1920–2012
Ethel May Garlepp	1909–1997	Mary Agnes Garlepp	1898–1961
Eva Agnes GARLEPP	1893–1957	Mary Ellen Garlepp	1889–1941
Freda Violet Myrtle Garlepp	1918–1998	Mary GARLEPP	1894–1894
fritz Garlepp	1851–1851	Michael Charles Garlepp	1951–2020
George Henry Garlepp	1874–1919	Nancy Patricia Garlepp	1930–
George Patrick Garlepp	1891–1954	Nellie Murial Olive Garlepp	1913–1988
George Patrick Garlepp	1918–1978	Pam Garlepp	
George Patrick Garlepp	1919–1978	Patricia Garlepp	
Gloria 'Betty' Mena GARLEPP	1918–2015	Robert Garlepp	
Henry (Heinrich) Garlepp	1861–1916	Robert Morris (Bob) Garlepp	1931–2023
Henry Garlepp	1894–	Sarah Ann Garlepp	1893–1979
Hermann GARLEPP	1859–1931	Sharon Garlepp	
Hugh Theodore Garlepp	1896–1957	Thelma Garlepp	1936–1936
Ivy Agnes Garlepp	1911–1980	Thomas George Garlepp	1928–1999
Janice Ann Garlepp	1939–2018	Trevor Russell Garlepp	1943–2004
Jocelyn Garlepp	1934–	Veronica Mavis Garlepp	1912–1933
John Barry Garlepp	1937–2010	Violet Lily Myrtle Garlepp	1898–

Wayne Garlepp	
Wilhelm GARLEPP	1856–1898
William Austin Garlepp	1908–1982
William George Garlepp	1887–1964
William Patrick Garlepp	1915–
William Roy Garlepp	1915–1998
Martin Friedrich Gerlipp Dr	1787–1840
Ellen Agnes GREENWOOD	1864–1927
Christina Dorothea Friederike Maria Johanne Gunther	1853–1941
Thelma Irene Halliday	1910–2007
Minnie Elsie Hansen	1913–2004
Agnes Harnden	1915–1988
Clara Maud Harnden	1888–1982
Edward Harnden	1924–1999
Ellen Kathleen Harnden	1908–1961
Ellen Mary Harnden	1926–2002
Ernest Spencer Harnden	1930–2016
George Patrick Harnden	1918–1987
Harry Harnden	1920–1995
James Henry Spencer Harnden	1910–1972
James Spencer Harnden	1884–1972
John Joseph (Jack) Harnden	1922–2004
Patricia Nancy Harnden	1928–2013
William Edward Harnden	1912–1936
Henry Carrum Jones	1898–1985
Janette Elizabeth Jones	1952–2006
barry john Kennaugh	
John Lewis Kennaugh	1914–
Cheryl Kiely	
Christine Kiely	
Glen Kiely	
Kenneth Raymond Kiely	1920–1985
James William Henry Little	1911–1952
James William LITTLE	1892–1964
Nellie Veneta LITTLE	1912–1982
Nellie Irene Matthews	1920–2014
Roy William Matthews	1894–1972
Charles Arthur May	1878–1939
Charles Clement May	1916–1976
Dorothy Helen May	–1982
Margaret May	1916–1981
Barrie Ronald McCole	–1994
Leslie Ralph McCole	1920–1994
Robyn Lesliegh McCole	1949–2007
Lillian May McCrory	1919–2016
Daisy McFadden	1895–1978
Gladys Mary McLennan	1917–1981
Brian Meehan	1948–1989
Dianne Marie Meehan	–1955
John Patrick Meehan	1947–1977
Patrick Joseph Meehan	1922–1969
Peter Anthony Meehan	1957–1991
Gladys Elizabeth Moffatt	1912–1995
Reuben Matthew Morrissey	1917–1993
Alma Veronica Neenan	1890–1949
Noeline Helen Otto	1945–2016
Jessie Stewart Ousley	1921–1968
Maxwell James Pinnell	1921–2000
Ethel May Robertson	1885–1954
Horace Charles Rosewarne	1908–1995
Thomas Charles Rosewarne	1935–2008
Grace Louise Shore	1895–1953
Sidney Edward Shore	1928–2019
Sidney Seymour Shore	1897–1971
Sophia Agnes (Patricia) Smith	1902–1968
Eve Christina Stubbs	1908–1989
Daniel Jas Tierney	1885–1957
Lorna May Tierney	1916–1995
Nellie Irene Tierney	1915–1915

William Henry Garlepp/Tierney	1909–1941
Donald Lawrence Tunes	1939–
Janice Marlene Tunes	1940–
Leslie John "Les" Tunes	1936–2016
Lillian Merle Tunes	1937–
Cyril Alexander Walker	1924–1924
Daniel Joseph Walker	1927–1927
David Alexander Walker	1887–1935
Donald Joseph Walker	1930–2020
John Walker	1929–
Leslie Walker	1923–
Lilian Walker	1934–
Agnes Myrtle Eldridge Waters	1921–1921
Ivy May Wiles	1915–1969